# PLANTING

## by the

# MOON

# Gilead

## Numbers: 32

Now the sons of Reuben and the sons of Gad had a very great multitude of cattle; and they saw the land of Jazer and the land of Gilead, and behold, the place was a place for cattle.

# PLANTING
## by the
# MOON

## On life in
## a mountain hamlet

## Peter Stillman

Boynton/Cook Publishers
HEINEMANN
Portsmouth, NH

Boynton/Cook Publishers

361 Hanover Street
Portsmouth, NH 03801-3912
*Offices and agents throughout the world*

**Library of Congress Cataloging-in-Publication Data**

Stillman, Peter
    Planting by the moon : on life in a mountain hamlet / Peter Stillman
        p. cm.
    ISBN 0-86709-347-1
    1. Mountain life--New York (State)--Catskill Mountain Region--Literary collections. 2. Catskill Mountains Region (N.Y.)--Social life and customs.    I. Title
    PS3569.T48213P53  1994
    818'.5403--dc20
    [B]                                              94-34646
                                                        CIP

Printed in the United States of America on acid-free paper
T & C Digital 2010

*For Jon, Dan and Tom,*
*who grew up to be good men*
*in this stony testing place.*

# Contents

Preface   ix

George's Place   1

Charlie's Place   35

The Mountain   73

# Preface

You won't find Gilead by studying a map of the Catskills. I've adopted the name because I like its sound, its mountained origin, and its allusive Biblical quality. Also, I'd just as soon keep Gilead's real name to myself. You get somewhat possessive about a small town you've grown to know and care deeply about. It takes a long time to understand such a place and to fit yourself somewhere into its complicated tapestry. Never mind that you've only borrowed for a millisecond of eternity the right to call it your own; it is for that moment uniquely, privately yours. Moreover, Gilead has remained largely undiscovered and hence ungentrified, and I'd rather it continued that way.

This little book doesn't attempt to explain life in a mountain hamlet. Nor is it a history, although Gilead has a rich one well worth writing about. What follows is one man's fumbling to know a place, to discover for himself how he feels about it. Like nearly any personal writing that attempts honesty, it is also unavoidably a discovery of oneself, for no two people ever truly see or feel anything the same way.

Much of the text derives from journals and letters written over a span of twelve years. Not that I've kept copies of my letters. That, I've always felt, is somehow dishonest. To my surprise and delight, though, others had been saving what I'd sent to them. From these hundreds of letters I culled a couple of dozen excerpts. The rest of the prose text is parts of journal entries. No distinction is made between one and the other.

The poems are relatively recent. I wrote most of them in 1981, or began to. Poems, even fairly light ones such as these, are never truly finished, only, as French poet Paul Valery once observed, "abandoned." Most of them have been published elsewhere; three or four appear here for the first time. A number of the poems are linked topically or thematically to prose pieces, although that was never part of any plan. I've often seen my words veer off from prose to poetry and back again, and there is no accounting for it; when you pick up a pencil, anything can happen.

The pieces don't follow a tight chronological order. Thus, it may help to know that when I moved to Gilead in 1971, it was into George's rickety old house on the corner. About six years later I bought Charlie's place, the one the poplar fell on. Three years after that I built a cabin on a remote section of Winthrop Foote's farm above Gilead.

The general store I write about has been closed for years, and George, Charlie, Bill, and Everett are long dead. To a very occasional visitor, much would appear to have changed over the span of time that concerns me here. At heart, however, it is still the same Gilead, stubbornly unlike any other community on earth. (Once a woman from a town much closer to sea level condescendingly called me "one of those mountain people from Gilead," and I tingled with pride.)

I've changed some people's names, more from whim than necessity. The issue isn't who these people really are, anyhow; it's whether something of them seems alive and interesting to you. Nobody in here is a fiction, by the way, and nowhere have I put corny-quaint *Reader's Digest* rusticisms into anyone's mouth.

Originally, this preface was to have concluded with a paragraph or so about how much I care about the fine, tough people of Gilead and the hills that hem them in. But if the book conveys what I mean it to, such comments should not be necessary; the affection will show.

&

I wrote that preface ten years ago when this book, much of it at least, was first published in a limited edition funded by the New York State Council on the Arts. It was originally titled Gilead.

I moved away from the hamlet about then and lived elsewhere for ten years. For the roughly four thousand days of my absence, I ached to return. I didn't realize how much, however, until I began poring through letters and journal entries in preparation for this edition. For stretches they are passionate with longing. Here's part of one:

I drove down to Gilead yesterday afternoon. I love to pause at the head of the valley and look down the narrow winding road and pretend I have never entered it before, that I do not know I will come upon a nondescript little community five miles to the west. I never tire of seeing Gilead for the first time. There are more mobile homes dotting the valley's flanks now, most of them ill-tended, and Otto's place is an even more wretched mess. But there is so much beauty to this valley that I can take in the ugliness at a skim, perceive its particulars to be casual trash dropped in the wake of a storm.

After my visit, Bing and I stand outside in his yard. He presses me to come back soon, and suddenly I am so flooded with memories that I can't speak. Instead I nod yes and start up the little slope toward the road. I look out over his flat and remember turning it with his father's old John Deere and planting potatoes; and how one March I tried crossing the creek down there on horseback, and the animal flung itself into the deepest pool; and how we'd sit

*xi*

evenings on Bing's never-to-be-finished deck talking endlessly about nothing and watching deer come down and cross. I turn around and say to him, "Please don't ever leave this place."

"Well," he says, "we looked around some, but no. Prob'ly stay here 'til we die."

I run down to Bobby's even though it's getting late. He's making up a stove for boiling. I ask him how the sapping's been and I'm surprised when he says it hasn't been a good year, that he and the boys haven't even checked his tanks for over a week. "Guess we'll gather for the last time tomorrow," he says, and I'm touched for a second by the ironic melancholy of his words.

"I don't want to get going about it, but I sure miss this place," I say to him.

"You can fix that easy enough," Bobby answers. "Move back."

So that's what I did.

Peter Stillman

# I

# GEORGE'S PLACE

## Two Ways In

You who come
by way of the hill
see first the stream—
in August piebald cows
cool their udders in its pools—
and then a hollow field,
and only then the town.
You've come the way
the deer slip down.

The other way
is through the valley,
and where the town begins,
the hay is tangled and uncut,
and wire too old to stop
a cow is all that holds
the leaning fence in place.
By such proximity
is beauty often marred.
This way in
the sights are hard.

I was out early this morning prying loose three sets of axles that had settled over the years into the barnyard sod and rooted there. In the midst of heaving and straining I got to thinking about George Murfitt. He was the most aphoristic fellow I've ever known, although I doubt he ever realized the knack he had or sculpted his pronouncements in the privacy of his head before uttering them. He, like his fellow countryman Samuel Johnson, had the great and natural gift of pithiness, a way of getting right to the bottom of things without wasting words. I told him one Saturday that I was going to run down to Cobleskill to buy some tool or other and did he need anything from the hardware store. He said no he didn't, but then he went right on to say that I didn't either. Another knack George had was for slowing you down when he knew you were in a hurry. "The one tool a man needs to get through life," he told me, "is a crowbar."

I said I didn't see how I could use a crowbar to redecorate the bathroom in his terrible old house and he said he didn't know either and that's why he'd left it the way it was. "If you can't do it with a crowbar, the devil with it," he explained and turned and went inside.

George had left his bar in the woodshed when he moved across the road. It was the biggest one I'd ever seen, nearly as tall as I am and meant for heavy business. When I reminded him that he'd forgotten to take it, he said he hadn't forgotten, that he'd left it there in the hope it would put some sense in my head. George has been dead for years now, and I still don't know what he meant about crowbars, but it's the one tool I own that I'm even faintly sentimental about. If I moved into a high-rise tomorrow, I'd take it with me.

❧

### SOME OF THE OLD

Some of the old
burn the trash in the dooryard
and stand in the thick
of the smoke.
I always wave.
Some wave back.
Because they still
plant by the moon I wave.
Because they named
their useless sons for kings
and never spend or touch
and keep without a book.

4

Because they write
in the wild script
of the poor I wave. Because
some widows wear
a husband's coat and let
the stove go cold.

## ON RESTORATION

Last weekend I patched the wooden cover over the dug well
that supplies us with water. The job changed from a simple
chore to an exercise in Poe-like frenzy when someone pointed out that I had better seal up all the cracks so that mice,
rats, toads, and snakes would have no way to fall into the
well and drown. The final job calls attention to itself not
because it appears to be a neatly repaired well cover, but
rather a hermetically sealed tomb. Nor was I able for a couple of days to turn on a faucet without expecting corroded
bits of reptile to plop into the sink.

I need two thousand used bricks to build the chimney.
Everett mentioned that he'd heard about a couple of sources.
Knowing something of value to another grants him a feeling
of great self-importance, although he has no sense of respon-
sibility about the accuracy of his information. Thus, it was
with some distrust that I set off with him to scout for bricks.

Our first stop was just up the hill at the Mitchell place.
They own the largest red setter I've ever seen. Elsie came out
on the porch, which was vibrating from the furious lungings
of the chained and howling animal. She told me that sometimes the dog doesn't bite but that it's impossible to tell when

he will or won't. Anyhow, she didn't have any bricks on the place. "Tell Everett he's crazy," she said. "Last week I asked *him* where we could find some."

Everett had sat calmly through our visit, smoking his pipe and chatting with himself. I said, "Why did you tell me she had bricks?"

"Dunno," he answered. "Heard her say somethin' about 'em."

Our next stop was at Mrs. Wilson's place. "Won't git me in there," Everett said. "Old witch's got a hunnerd thirty-two cats, and ever' one's leapin' with fleas."

Mrs. Wilson, an ancient and wobbly widow, looked puzzled when I asked her about bricks. "Who told you I had bricks?" she asked. "Everett," I said. "Well you tell that little bugger for me to get down here and split my wood, or I'll take a cane to him. Bricks! I've got maybe ten of them down the barn. Tell you, though, you can have all the rocks you want, so long as you haul them away."

Everett was cowering in the car, having slid out of sight the moment Mrs. Wilson opened her door. I thanked her for offering me her rocks, listened politely while she explained how God made daffodils, and then dropped Everett off at his shack.

George's device for exiting from the back door was not only grotesque and dangerous, it was also exotic. Over the years he had strung together a series of shaky platforms of decreasing height. They looked much less like stairs than the kind of flimsy constructions Indians fling up to spear fish from. When walked upon they wobbled and tipped, for they were neither attached to each other nor squared with the ground. I asked George why he had built such an ugly, hazardous contraption rather than a set of stairs.

"They work perfectly," he told me. "Besides, the only one who used that door was Ethel, not counting the cats.

And I've never lived in a place where she didn't fall down-stairs at least once a month, so you can see it wouldn't have made any difference to her."

I asked him if Ethel had ever fallen off his platforms. "Yes, of course. Regularly."

When I mentioned to Charlie that I was going to build a set of stairs, he told me that he'd much rather I put up a whole rear deck. There is no arguing with him about such matters; he's always right. "I'll build a little landing and extend it some day," I told him.

"It'll only cost you more that way," he answered, destroying my one effort at pretended practicality.

Charlie sat on a sawhorse in the shade and directed the project, calling out altered dimensions as he read from my original plans. It occurred to me that afternoon for the twen-tieth time that the spirit underlying nearly all my desperate restoration activities is being guided and controlled by him and George. The latter must be gratified, the former satis-fied. Together they form a nearly total being: George is very much the emotional force to which I'm answerable, while Charlie is the logic. There is little room for me in the mix, which may be for the better. Left to my own devices, I'd lie in the shade. The deck was in place by six that night. Charlie, visibly exhausted, left his perch and went home for dinner.

🐂

Rotted timbers: Any book on restoration is unequivocal about the need to banish all signs of rot from a house. The imperative, one gathers from experts, transcends practical considerations and enters the realm of higher ethics: rot is bad. Not like a leaky roof, a warped door, but like a social disease. Rot in a house isn't merely a sign of old age, damp-ness, and genteel neglect; it is a disgrace no less than being father of the town whore. Rip out the rot before your neigh-

7

bors hear about it; exorcise it before it snatches your children's souls.

I've developed a less Puritanical view. The first main timber I exposed was rotten to the core. An entire corner of the house, I discovered, was about to collapse into the basement. Yet I had to fight the dark urge to slap something over the punky beam simply to avoid a scandal. Instead, I jacked up the corner and replaced it. To my horror, I discovered that the next beam was rotten too, and that fitting a new one in its place would involve major construction. So instead I attacked it, more in a frenzy of anger than in any hope of salvaging it. After two days of chiseling, though, I reached sound wood, saturated the thing with preservative and left it there. What remains is six inches thick and a foot wide. Find me a modern house constructed of timbers that beefy.

I'll never replace another bad beam. Rot travels slowly, and why should a man care what happens to a structure after he has collapsed into his own basement? Nail a 6 x 6 next to it and the hell with it. Talk openly to your neighbors, the bank, the family about the *one* bad beam you uncovered and replaced. This will convey a healthy, two-fisted kind of grit and strength of character on which the American myth is built.

There are at least thirty bird nests in various crannies of the house. A wren can squeeze into a hole no larger across than a quarter, and our place is riddled with quarter-sized holes. Wasps live in the dime-sized ones, which is okay with me. They're not belligerent, and I'm willing to respect their modest territorial demands. Furthermore, they're neat and quiet, much unlike the average wren. I've read that nests must be removed from the hollows of a house. They're a fire and health hazard. Nesting materials promote rot; droppings stain paint; and chirping, squawking, and flapping noises are a nuisance. Destroy the nests, seal up the entryways, discourage by means fair or foul any feathered wildlife from taking up residence in your house. So the experts say.

It is, of course, a contemptible act to destroy a home filled with helpless young. Last week, while painting the east wing, I unwittingly came within inches of a hidden nest. The mother wren became so agitated that she turned to infanticide, throwing her newly hatched babies out of the second-story hole. I wasted two hours stuffing them back in, but as fast as I did, she fired them out again. Meanwhile, Ethel, George's wife, stood at the foot of the ladder shouting instructions and shooting black looks at me. It was an insufferable experience.

My advice to the restorer: Don't even consider painting and patching an old house during nesting season. The way is not clear; one cannot do a decent job while fettered with complex moral restraints. Wait 'til the birds leave and demolish their nests right down to the last straw. Done with stealth and swiftness, it leaves one answerable only to himself.

### BREAK-IN OIL

Earl said she'd only kind of
run away. Took off in the Impala
after he'd just done the valves
and rings. Never said a word.
She did things by halves, Wanda—
nearly pretty, sort of smart
in school, fooled around a little,
married Earl.

9

Ordell Haines left too, but he'd
do that, so there wasn't any talk,
except he'd probably head for Florida
again, 'til someone said
she'd mentioned going there
and California too before she died.
And if Ordell went alone, how come
he didn't take the truck?

Wanda called her sister up from
Baltimore, said she hadn't
left, just gone off. Then
her other one from outside
Chattanooga, then the first again
from Arkansas somewhere. You
could see from looking at a map
she couldn't make her mind up.
Earl was sick about her driving
all that way on break-in oil.
Then she more or less came back.
(Ordell did too, but he stayed three
towns over for a week.) The right
front fender was banged up,
her hair was different-colored,
and there were things she said
she'd never do again, including the
pigs and giving it to Earl whenever
he said. Not putting on airs,
just letting you know there was
something to her after all.

The little homemade booklet we found inside the parlor wall
must be about a century old. It's a repository of home remedies, some for afflictions I've never heard of. "Duality of cir-

10

culation," for example: according to the notes, it is "the cause of fever disturbances of the vital or nervous circulation." What you do for it is take syrup of stillingia, camphor water, and morphine, one teaspoon at a time. Probably a person could get through life on a remedy like that, regardless of the contrary ways his blood is pumping. Pleurisy is treated with opium, emphysema with green lobelia. Other remedies call for belladonna and chloroform, with cinchonine being recommended as a "brain tonic."

Set off by themselves as if they weren't fit to mingle with man's run-of-the-mill miseries are "RX for rattle snake bites," "RX for the bite of mad dog," and "Syphilis perscription." You can't help but muse about the relative incidence of these problems a hundred years back. No one I know has ever seen a rattler in these parts (although everybody's grandfather killed a twenty-footer when he was a boy). As for mad dogs and syphilis, I'd guess there would be one or the other running around town every once in a while. For snake bite you take a mixture of gunpowder and whiskey; if a dog gets you, it's strychnine and nicotine; but for syphilis the one legible ingredient is lime or lavender water. Given a choice of afflictions, there would seem to be only one sensible way to go.

PARTING TWICE

A winter death means parting twice.
No irony attends: the land's
in ice too hard and deep
for digging graves, but sorrow's green
and will not keep; we congregate
to whisper in stuffy rooms
hired out for grief.

Come spring a hearse will haul
the fellow up the hill, and we,
with leafing all around, will meet
to say some drier words
and see him in the ground.

There's a long ladder here in the valley—Jessup's ladder. It doesn't belong to Jessup anymore and hasn't for some years. Still, it's known as Jessup's ladder, much as the house I bought is still George Murfitt's place. It will be the obligation of whoever inherits the thing to lend it out, for it is, after all, the longest ladder around. I borrowed it from Gaius Vroman because I needed it to paint the high peak of the main wing. Setting it up was an awful job; it must weigh over a hundred pounds. Twice it fell on me, once when the frizzled old manila line broke. But I got it finally into place and took a practice climb without bucket or brush. I stood on the third rung from the top and waved my arm around in a painting motion. The ladder took a sudden lurch to the left and began to slip. I scrabbled at the siding, the trim, the slanted edge of roof, and when the hitching stopped and I dared a look, I could see that one of the legs was an inch or so off the ground. After what seemed an hour, I ventured a first terrified step to a lower rung and, tilting hard to the right, made my way down without incident.

I sat on the grass and tried to loosen for a bit and thought not about how to secure the ladder or otherwise how to reach that towering section, but instead about the old, paint-splattered monster leaning askew on my shabby house. How many times had men from this valley—farmhands, homeowners, builders—scaled its highest rungs simply because they had to? How many siloes, barns, houses had it been propped against? How long would it last? When would a rung go, a rail break, a pulley rip out? Not

12

now, not this time, I told myself. There had to be another day in it, another safe climb. I jammed a flat piece of shale under the unbalanced leg, took up bucket and brush and climbed again.

George Murfitt must have been watching from his window across the road. Before I'd taken the first stroke he was at the foot of the ladder telling me no one would notice that section of the house anyway and to get down before I killed myself. I refused, said it had to be done, and he said that if I insisted on being a bloody fool he would at least hold the ladder. He had little faith in himself as anchor man, however, and went on morbidly about people falling from roofs and siloes and ladders over the years. He even related a significant dream that had reconciled him to death. "I had always been terrified of dying, until one night not more than a year ago I dreamt that I was walking a narrow path which led to a precipice. I was sick with fright because I knew I must walk over its edge. Suddenly, a presence appeared and pointed to the brink. I turned, saluted in military fashion, and walked off."

He let go of the ladder and saluted crisply. It bucked once and skidded four inches to the right. "Grab it!" I screamed, again scrabbling for a handhold. He looked proudly up at me and said, "I've not been afraid of death since." Then he cautioned me not to leap around so much up there, repeated his observation that it was foolish to paint an out-of-the-way spot, and returned to holding the ladder.

The back of the house is about a foot higher than the front. Next weekend I'll reborrow Jessup's ladder and go at it, without benefit of dream.

## COMING DOWN FROM LUTHERANVILLE

Eddy said Joe Koker said
when he came down from Lutheranville,
what struck him was the chicken houses
lighted up at night. He said he took
them for a city, lights blazing up
and down the road. "I thought I'd made
a wrong turn at the crossing. I thought
I'd drove into a city filled with big
hotels. It scared me for a minute."
Eddy tells good stories. He's the last
one left. Old Joe was second-to-the-last.

Anyhow, the incident with Jessup's ladder got me thinking about ladders in general and how they tend to transcend ownership and prop themselves here and there around the community where they're truly needed, not where they are meant by title to reside. Furthermore, a sort of proprietorship sets in after a person has lived with a borrowed ladder for a while; it doesn't seem quite right to give it back.

Years ago, I borrowed an aluminum stepladder from Sven. The longer I lived with it, the more uses it served, until it became indispensable enough so that only an idiot would have returned the thing. When, after all, had I ever seen Sven up on it? Why, it was barely used when I took it, and in just two or three years, I'd dented and bent it and splattered paint all over it—used it for what the Lord intended ladders to be used for. Moreover, if Sven ever did think to put it to some purpose of his own, all he had to do was walk across the road and ask to borrow it back.

So I kept it through the move to Charlie's place and found more uses for it over there. When I migrated to the

14

mountain, though, I left it in the barn, a sissy aluminum ladder being clearly out of place in such a rugged setting and far too short anyhow for working on the cabin. For that I borrowed Winthrop's eight-footer, a grand old wooden affair I'd have trusted in a full gale. I held on to it too; you can't find stepladders like that anymore. Furthermore, Winthrop and Esther's place has low ceilings; it didn't make a speck of sense for them to have a ladder that long.

About two years after I borrowed it, I stopped at their farm and caught Esther at window washing, and darned if she wasn't standing on my aluminum ladder—well, not exactly mine, Sven's, but as I had discovered, a person develops a covetousness about the things, and so I said, "That's my ladder you're standing on."

She said she knew it but I had theirs, so she figured it was only right she had mine and that's why she'd asked Bobby to borrow it. Bobby, though, never borrows anything. "He stole it," I said. "Same as he stole my hen and my cabbage slicer and the go-devil I bought from him for five dollars that I watched him steal from somebody else."

We left it that way. Wimp and Esther have Sven's ladder, which they refer to as Peter's, and I have theirs, which I refer to as mine. All of which came to mind just the other day when it occurred to me that if I can get Eddy to nail just one piece of siding on the front of the cabin—the high side—I'll have accomplished pretty much what I want, which is to get Milton's thirty-footer up to my place. I've wanted that ladder for ten years now. It's the only one left in Gilead tall enough to reach where I have to get. Eddy borrowed it from Milton four years ago, when he started working on his dead father's place, but actually from Mabel and Wayne, one of whom died and the other fled the Valley, and who got it from Milton way back because Mabel was Milton's sister-in-law's mother. I thought I'd seen the last of it when Mabel died because Bob, being Milton's brother and married to Jenny, who is Mabel's daughter, fell in love with it and would have dragged it back to Albany if he wasn't terrified of scratching up the roof of his Cadillac.

Late in the night of December 27 the fire siren went off. It is a terrible sound to wake to—raw, ugly, insistent. I don't, this time, have to wonder what or where the blaze is. As I hurry into clothing and boots in the dark of the living room, I see the awful brightness of open flame in the windows of a small, shabby house diagonally across the road. In the approximately two minutes it takes me to dress and dash out the door, the front of the place erupts in a sheet of fire, and blazing pieces of siding and shingles loft in the wind, come floating down on nearby rooftops.

The firehouse is just across the way, and as I run up, engines are coughing to life, men are throwing on turnout gear, snatching up equipment, stringing hoses from pumper to house. Despite the proximity, it is already too late; the fire has gotten to the house's vitals.

It's about five degrees above zero; even the men who are properly dressed suffer miserably, for we fight the thing until nearly 4:30, joined by others from three nearby districts. When we're done, we've emptied six tankers and a large pond. One of our trucks has blown its pump, four hoses have frozen and ruptured, a score of firefighters have been injured or sickened by smoke. The Rescue Squadron ambulance from Summit has been standing by most of the night, dispensing oxygen and first aid. My coat is sheathed with ice; whenever I've been relieved, I've stood by shaking uncontrollably. Others are in similar condition. The Women's Auxiliary passes out coffee and donuts, and Butch has thought to run whiskey down from his tavern.

It has been a grim night's work but somehow stirring too. I don't like fires and wouldn't walk around the corner to see one. Always after a big, nasty blaze, though, I get a funny lump in my throat. There's no way to put it without sound-

16

ing softheaded. You'd have to be there in the dark, hanging onto a bucking three-inch, high-pressure hose, slipping on the ice forming underfoot, moving closer and closer into the stinking, searing ugliness of a fire, gagging on the smoke, taking back into your face, your collar and sleeves most of the stale, frigid water that bounces from the walls and roof, to know how powerfully you begin to love the black-coated fellow next to you. I can't explain the intimacy—why, even after the fire is out, men linger, despite the hour, the drenched and reeking clothes, the exhaustion—why they are reluctant to go home. It never fails to touch me.

### VFD

The siren fits itself to dream at first,
the way a lip of cold will seem a kiss.
But now the rising moan is flame itself,
and old men wake and listen to it crack low
    stars,
while lost in smoke as thick as sleep,
we lean the ladders close and climb,
and shouts fly out like valiant sparks
and tumble down the January night.

In a village not far from here things have come to a boil. According to this morning's paper, firemen and ambulance teams have formally resolved not to respond to alarms connected with "emergencies at Viola Albanese's house."

Mrs. Albanese's neighbors have responded in somewhat similar fashion. At the town board meeting where the fire and rescue units presented their resolution, board members also received a petition from seventeen local residents that reads: "We appeal to you, the board members, not to allow a tragedy to occur before you take action on this matter."

It's no small thing for a community to become so perturbed that they resort to terms like *tragedy* and where they move to deny a citizen protection from fire or other calamity. Such extremes of sentiment don't square with what we like to think about smalltown America. Still, as a volunteer fireman, I go along with the VFD over there. Mrs. Albanese keeps an African lion on her premises, and I would no more go crashing through the door of a lion-infested house than I would wrestle an alligator or vote Republican.

There are at least two sides to the issue, however. Mrs. Albanese also attended the meeting, along with her daughter Joan. Joan has a lion, too, named Kittycat. (Mrs. Albanese calls her lion Baby.) In response to the fire and ambulance squad's position that they "will not go on any calls as long as a lion is harbored on the premises," Joan observed with some heat, "Great! You tell us if our house burns down, us and our kids can burn in there and you won't lift a drop of water to stop it."

Mrs. Albanese averred that should a fireman break down her door with an ax, Baby would probably run and hide. She is after all, only a youngster of about two hundred fifty pounds, half of what she'll weigh full-grown, given her current diet of four pounds of raw chicken a day. As for Kittycat's whereabouts, Joan was understandably cagey. Only recently, another village had virtually run her and her lion out of town. "[They] gave me a shafting that was unbelievable," she said. "They not only knocked me down, they kicked me when I was down there."

The town Supervisor accused Joan of "not being very cooperative" for failing to come clean about where the second lion is. To his credit, however, he also established that he wants any ordinance coming out of the dispute to be "right and fair" to all involved. He didn't say whether or not that included Baby and Kittycat.

We've had numerous disputes over the years about animals here in Gilead, although none of this magnitude. It's part of life in a rural community. Once in a while a bull will get loose and do some damage, and just last year, Milton accused two of my horses of defecating on his brother's grave.

The most recent issue involved a woman who rented a falling-down cottage and stuffed it full of mangy dogs, about twenty-five of them, according to Ralph, her neighbor, who finally got so agitated about their howling that he crashed his Buick through her front porch and into her kitchen. He was charged on three counts: driving an unregistered vehicle, malicious property damage, and assault with intent to do bodily harm. He pleaded guilty to the first two charges but not the third. I happened to be there when he told the Justice that the idea of inflicting simple bodily harm had never crossed his mind. "I wanted to fix her and her damn dogs for good," he explained.

I read in last Sunday's *New York Times* a review about a new book on sex education. The author recommends explaining to children that the father places his sperm in the mother approximately the same way four-footed animals do. That might suffice in a city setting, where kids rarely see anything natural happening anyway, but up here such information could lead to the bizarre image of Dad howling and urinating all over the porch until Mom throws herself through the screen door and they go at it, lathered up and blank-eyed, in the middle of the road. Kids step right over copulating dogs and chickens here without paying them any mind. Tell them that's how they got their start in the world, though, and it would probably rattle them pretty badly.

## GAIUS CONKLIN'S TOOLS

When Gaius Conklin died, his son
came into all his tools,
a cellarful of chisels, files,
planes and saws; a grindstone, draw-
knives, braces, awls. . .
and Henry lugged them up the narrow stairs.
"I don't know that I'll do
with most of these," he said.
"There's some were old before my father's
    time."

In sunlight all had gained a bulk
and lost the look of use.
No glint was in the steel; what shone
were handles worn to fit
another's grip. But here such things
aren't thrown away. What's old
is saved to fix what's old.

The boxes went to Henry's barn
and filled a corner of the empty loft.
But Henry's wife is not the kind
to let things be. She rummages.
She pulled a spoke-shave from
the clutter, wired it to a beam
and from it hung a Boston fern.
Within a week she'd fastened to
a parlor wall a dozen other tools,
from mallet to auger to adze.
One by one old grim-edged implements
were nailed or propped in every room,
and Henry's Christmas gift that year
was a hickory-handled plane
converted to a table lamp.

In March we helped to butcher Henry's hog,
and later in the kitchen Eddy joshed,
"Your father's likely spinning in
his grave, the way you've turned his tools
to ornaments."

"I guess she's got a right
to pretty up the place," was all
that Henry said.

I've never known a milder man.
Thus, Easter Sunday's rumor that
there'd been a row up there
provoked my curiosity.

I found him in the barn, his shirt
stained dark with sweat, the floor
a litter of his father's tools
and shavings from a crooked beam.
He paused to eye his edge. "That plane,"
I asked. "Isn't that the one. . .?"

"I needed it," he said. "I've let
this barn go long enough.
Another winter she'll come down."

"I have a plane like that. You
could've borrowed mine."

"Why should I?" Henry answered. "This
one works just fine."

21

Yesterday was one of those ineffably lovely Sundays in May when, regardless of what their own plans may have been, children get pushed into the family car and taken for a ride. Even those without automobiles succumb: at about noon Julius, shaved and looking spiffy, came down the road on his bright red tractor towing his entire family and Gordon in a manure spreader. They all waved gaily from their lawn chairs as as they went by, and although you must imagine otherwise, it was an entirely pretty and heartwarming little spectacle.

Our local capitalist used to pay Everett twenty-five cents an hour to sit and listen to him play the violin. Whenever he picks up his fiddle, the family clears out. Everett, who'll tolerate nearly anything, finally quit, said he couldn't stand it anymore. "Twice I asked him for a raise, but he just shook his head and kept on scrapin' away. I never had a worse job in my life!"

Everett's fits are only partly legitimate, according to Charlie. He told me that Everett would have a fit once or twice a year, whenever it occurred to him, until he happened to be stricken in front of the home of two old ladies who live just down the road. Greatly concerned, they picked him up, carried him into the house, put him to bed and fed him. That ruined him, Charlie said. After that he'd have two or three fits a week, always just outside the ladies' house—sometimes right up on the porch so they wouldn't have to drag him so far.

The last time I visited Winthrop and Esther, he told me about how just before the War, Dolph Van Hoosen finally gave in to the times and sold his team and bought a tractor.

"Dolph wasn't much for machinery, but he knew enough to get her started. Then he pointed her at the first field up on the high flat back of Helen and Larry's used to belong to the Swedes, and off he went. He come at the corner of that field movin' at a pretty good clip, but all he did to slow her down was lean back some on the seat, which didn't mean anything to the tractor, of course. So what's he do then but stand up, haul back on the wheel and start shoutin' 'Whoa, dammit, whoa!'

"Didn't do a bit of good. Tractor climbed over the stone wall fence and kept goin'. Made a road for itself right down the middle of his cornlot, Dolph still hollerin' 'Whoa' at the top of his lungs."

❧

## MORE OR LESS

Old Thompson said that once
to woo a girl he told her,
"I love you for your yellow hair
and how it sets me wondering
what's underneath your dress."

A little more, I offered, might
have won her. But he,
who'd thought about it sixty years,
said no,
a little less.

❧

23

One of the most enduring symbols of rural America has nearly disappeared from this hamlet. The derelict cars that cankered many dooryards have almost all been cut up for scrap. There are those, however, who haven't given in to the high price being paid by salvage yards. My neighbor, Rooney, has hung on to all eight of his wrecks. One is for his dogs to sleep in. They're chained to the axle of a 1958 Pontiac. Another is for his chickens, who live in a Dodge panel truck with a run built off the side. The rest of his junk vehicles he keeps because they have some special meaning for him. He is, for example, sentimentally wrapped up in the chassis of a three-quarter ton pick-up which stands sentinel-like on end by his back door. "Bought that baby brand new when we got married. Four hundred thousand miles on her," he told me, fondly slapping a frame rail. Apparently his wife feels similarly. She once referred to the chassis as "Old Red." Rooney just purchased a new car, a small foreign model that he parks partly in their summer kitchen.

After a year here, I still don't know how many children the Rooneys have, mainly because they're never let out of the house as a group, but only one at a time. I do sense that they're all named Robert, except Roberta, the daughter. They're good neighbors. Rooney shot his brother-in-law last Memorial Day for attacking me with a baseball bat, which was a wonderfully thoughtful gesture from someone I'd just gotten to know. It was only a superficial leg wound, but it took the steam clear out of the fellow. The trooper who investigated told Rooney that next time he should use a larger caliber weapon and aim about a foot and a half higher.

From the *Gilead Valley News*, November 1878:
"A man who will take a newspaper for three or four years and not pay for it, will pasture a goat on the grave of his grandfather."

24

The geese are going over. We're in the path of one of the great migratory flyways the big Canadas follow. How noble they look up there, strung out in long, undulating strands. Higher than any scanning hawk they come, moving at forty to fifty miles an hour, gabbling incessantly, shifting patterns and leaders, forging southward ever, staying airborne sometimes for twelve to fifteen hours at a time, riding the thin sky on thirty thousand beats of those broad gray wings. And now they pass over Gilead, and the land below them burns in autumn beauty. No one, desperately busy or preoccupied as he may be, can fail to stand and watch in awe the coming of wild geese.

On this last, storm-fraught day of May, I came upon a scene that so delighted me I want to carry it always at the edge of my memory. At about four, I left for the post office. Just past the bend at the head of the hill, I noticed something in the alfalfa lot. I pulled to a stop and backed up. It was what I had thought, two red fox kits sitting primly in the rain. They were perhaps fifty feet from the dense hedgerow, where almost certainly there is a den. I sat in the truck watching them watch me, then exited slowly from the passenger-side door, hunkering low and making the fox call I learned as a kid, the sound of a wounded rabbit, produced by drawing air through pursed lips so that it makes a high-pitched squeal.

Neither moved as I approached, until finally the near one broke, dashing into the hedgerow. It was too curious to stay hidden, however. The sound and the odd, lumbering creature drew it back, first the elegant little muzzle poking out of the brush, then the head, with its over-sized, black-fringed ears, then the rest of it, bounding into the open. The other one had continued to sit, seemingly unperturbed, until I came so

25

close—within a yard—that she, too, streaked for cover. Just before she did, I knelt in the mud and said, "I give this earth back to you."

### YESVEMBER

Yes comes
from places
in the sky
and settles. Two
brown leaves
rasp it. Geese
whistle *yes*
down a pale wind.

Snow is letters.
I let
the y's and e's and esses
sting my eyes,
and taste their
cold agreements on my tongue.

Gilead Creek meanders generally southward toward the Susquehanna. For most of the year its course is indecisive; occasionally in a dry summer it quits along the way. But come late March and into April it's a roarer, hellbent for big water. Twice I've nearly drowned a son in it trying to make a run in a kayak too long and unwieldy to swing the sudden, narrow bends.

Jon and I got only as far as Dibble's pasture the first time. We were ripping along hooting in pure joy when we came up on a rock, the stream breaking over it and spuming six feet in the air. Within a couple of seconds we were up to our necks in water so cold and belligerent it was a toss-up whether we'd freeze or drown first. We fought our way to the bank, picked up what was left of the craft, and squished home. Jon swore it was the last time he'd go adventuring with me, but he'd said that a dozen times before. A boy who'll take a green, one-eyed horse over a five-foot stone wall would, I knew, be game enough to try again.

Dan wasn't aware of the hazards of white water, so when I suggested on the third day of April that we shoot the creek, he agreed without hesitation. (When I'd talked about our possibly getting dunked, I made it sound [a] unlikely and [b] kind of fun.) We rendezvoused on the bridge five miles below the town. He had our kayak lashed to the top of his car, a larking look in his eye, and a six-pack of Bud ready to be swung aboard. He was obviously planning for a leisurely paddle. I didn't disabuse him.

It was three o'clock and about forty degrees when we put in, Dan in the bow. We hit the first bend going at a good clip. Directly in front of us a downed tree in the middle of a rip completely blocked the stream. There was no way by it, no time to swing for the bank. We hit bow on, the current whipping us broadside. Over we went, the open cockpit facing the surge.

Lord, it was cold! It tore the breath from our lungs, this snow-fed torrent from whose bankside vegetation shards of ice still clung. The current made standing nearly impossible, especially in water armpit deep. The kayak was jammed fast against the tree, trapped by countless tons of rushing stream. We had to shout over its roar, even though we were scant feet apart. "Told you we'd go in," I hollered, trying to inject a degree of cheer into the situation.

Somehow we worked the craft free and waded with it to the near bank. We had lost the spare paddle and a toolkit, but the beer had survived. "We'll quit after the third dunking," I said. One spill. . . by a slight stretch of the imagination, it could be taken as a harsh kind of fun. Males espe-

27

cially need ways to show their mettle, and what better circumstances than these, a frigid, booming creek, an unstable craft, a far, uncertain goal. I'll never outgrow my appetite for this kind of silly challenge and neither, I hope, will my sons. We portaged past the tree and put back in.

A mile or so later we ran aground just above a sharp bend where a towering jumble of stumps and branches had become anchored in midstream. There was room enough to get past the mess, but it would require some very adroit paddling. It was either take the chance or wade through a nasty stretch of swamp. "I don't think we'll make it," I said. Dan figured otherwise. What the hell; we'd warmed up by now, why not play the odds.

Maybe twenty seconds later, we slammed broadside into the tangle and capsized. I went completely under and Dan didn't fare much better. This is how paddlers drown, pinned underwater against a barricade of interwoven roots, branches, flotsam. Until one has been caught like this, it is impossible to comprehend how strong and implacable is the force of rushing water. Had either of us failed to grab an exposed limb, the chances of our meeting such a fate were excellent. Now we stood in water even deeper than before, the current tearing at us whenever we moved from the support of the long branches that held the kayak captive.

Again we broke the boat loose. Dan guided the partly submerged hull to the bank while I backtracked to retrieve flung paddles. He was shaking with the cold. The sun was lower now and so was the temperature. My wool fisherman's sweater kept me warm enough, even though it was soaked, but Dan had shed his parka. "Put it back on," I said. "Even wet it'll trap body heat." Then I asked him if he wanted to quit. But he said no, so we emptied out the kayak and put back in, this time settling into a long stretch of relatively easy water. Within half an hour we were reasonably comfortable again, hollering with glee when we hit rapids or swung a challenging bend.

I could sense in both of us, though, a growing fear of going in again. There was little sunlight left and we were getting worn. But we were happy, too. If all the trip had cost us was some lost gear and wet tobacco, it was a helluva buy. And there was the other matter as well: we had taken a ferocious beating, more than most men would have tolerated, and we were still afloat. When we had extricated the craft after the second spill, Dan grabbed my hand and gave it a squeeze. We did it, he meant.

We were still two miles short of our goal, the bridge at Butts Corners. We discussed pulling out early, perhaps at the old bridge by Brandow's farm. But when we got there, we decided to keep going. It was a mistake, our worst one. Just below Brandow's we hit heavy current again. It caught us unawares. Lulled by creeping exhaustion and cold, we boomed head-on into a huge jam formed by two downed trees that completely blocked our way. The kayak hit, inexorably tipping toward the current until the rushing water filled and buried it, its hull no more than a vague blue shadow beneath the dark current.

It was all too much. The sun was down, the air cold, the boat hopelessly trapped. We struggled with exhausted muscles against our gentle stream grown mighty, against the sodden weight of the submerged craft, the bullying, slippery stones underfoot. So strong was the press of water that a jutting branch tore through the kayak's deck. Maybe we should leave it here, I thought, catch a ride to the house, and return with the chainsaw. It was an agony to consider; it would be at least eight before we'd get back, and the thought of re-entering this ripping stream at that hour amounted to pure dread. Besides, there would be little of the kayak left to rescue by then; the chances were that it would be torn to pieces long before.

We broke loose a stout branch and used it for a pry, somehow finding strength enough to spring the boat loose once more. "That makes three dunks," I said. "We can quit with honor now, or we can take one more shot at getting there. It's up to you."

"I just don't want to go in again," Dan said. I didn't either. The prospect terrified me.

The last stretch wasn't bad, despite darkness. But when we finally reached the swimming hole above the bridge where we figured on pulling out, we discovered that it was a cauldron of roiling, spuming water. No matter how fiercely we paddled, the eddy would suck us away, drawing us ever closer to the dam beneath the bridge. Had we gone over, even if we stayed righted, we faced miles of black water far from any road or house. Anything but that.

We made at least eight passes at the shore, only to be spun back to midstream. Oh well, one of us commented, that's the way it goes some days. But we finally managed with the remnants of our collective energy to make one last stab at it, and it worked. The prettiest sound I heard that spring was our bow scraping shore.

It had been a folly every inch of the way. Unskilled and underprepared, I'd again put a son in danger. Nor could I claim that the venture had sprung from some ancient imperative, some worm in the brain that compels a father to push a fledgling into the perilous air. It had been a lark, something to attempt on an early April afternoon. Still, he'd been the one who had chosen to put back in that last time at Brandow's bridge. He hadn't even hesitated. Jon would have done the same. Tom, too. Good, tough boys, the lot of them. And past the cold on that last bridge, there was already a story forming in Dan's head. He'd get to tell it for the rest of his life.

A week before the annual horse show our VFD puts on, I realized that we needed cross-bars for the jumps. It was either buy them out of company funds, an unaffordable expense, or rummage through local scrap heaps hoping to find a dozen sound twelve-foot 4x4's, an unlikely prospect. Besides, time was too tight for scavenging. Why not use saplings, it occurred to me. Even painted they'd look inelegant, but that would more or less go with everything else— the sagging old haywagon we used for an announcer's stand, the snow fence ring, the road into the grounds so steep and rutted that most vehicles waited at the bottom for a tractor to tow them up.

I have a five-acre piece on Lape Road, most of it in scrawny maples, enough saplings to keep us in cross-bars well into the next century. I drove down to Bing's, who didn't subscribe to the crudely sexist maxim of local loggers: "Lend out your wife before your saw."
"You still got that little Homelite?" I said. Bing disappeared into his shop, rummaging and cursing for about twenty minutes, finally emerging with a chainsaw. "Still got some gas in her from when we tore down the porch," he said. It fired right up, too, so I poured in some bar oil, threw it in the back of the truck, and headed for the woods.

What you have to understand about chainsaws is that while they look mean enough to cut right through a tombstone, they're not. All it takes is hitting an old piece of barbed wire embedded in a tree or a nail holding up a porch, and the chain, which is racing around the bar at maybe ten thousand r.p.m., is suddenly, every last tooth, dull as a hoe. It should've taken ten minutes to knock down those saplings, maybe another ten or fifteen to trim them out. In half an hour I'd dropped two. An over-the-hill beaver could have bettered my time. But I was too deep in the woods to run back down to Gilead for a file, so I stuck at it, boiling mad at Cummings for palming off his next-to-useless saw on me.

It was the middle of a hot stretch, too, in the 90s and not a breath of breeze, even on the mountain. I quit for a spell, only half done. There's a little pond on the land, maybe sixty feet across, spring-fed and icy cold. I stood there sweating for a bit, then took off my clothes, walked down the slope and plunged in. It felt mighty pleasant. It had felt good just being naked, pushing through undergrowth toward water, even when branches and briars drew blood. Ten minutes in that pond and I emerged new, energized, knowing I had the job licked. I wasn't even angry with Bing anymore.

I didn't bother getting dressed. I felt a brute strength in my nakedness, a strength that clothing would have compromised. I cranked up the saw and set to it, never pausing to muse that nobody in the history of Gilead had ever before gone at chain-sawing buck naked. I did pause, though, halfway through the ninth sapling, to wipe the sweat from my eyes, the little blue machine guttering away in my hand.

There are any number of pains more excruciating than the one that occurs when the redhot manifold of an overworked chainsaw comes into contact with a naked thigh. To read up on them, however, requires going all the way back to the Old Testament. I felt the icy heat that serious burns convey, the eerie incandescence, heard the hiss of roasting flesh. I howled my way down to the slope, the saw still clutched insensibly in my hand. The water was my goal; it would drown the pain.

I burst out of the underbrush still screaming and onto the little patch of bare land that edges the pond. Two middle-aged women stood there. Both wore khaki safari jackets, primly long skirts, binoculars around their necks, and horrified looks. I stopped dead. One's instinct in such a circumstance is, of course, to cover oneself with whatever is available, so without thinking I swung Bing's still-idling saw to the front of me. The woman on the left clapped her hands over her eyes. The other one said, "Oh God, don't, please don't."

In an ecstasy of pain and mortification, I flung down the saw, bounded across the remaining yards and threw myself into the pond. I stayed under as long as my lungs would allow. When I surfaced, they were gone.

(This is the first time I've ever told this story and it'll probably be the last.)

# II

# CHARLIE'S PLACE

### LOOKER FOR LOOSE HORSES

Our horses trot stiff-legged at
the fence. Again they hear
what's calling in a wind and don't
belong to anyone, stare past
the hemming wire to some high place
where lookers for loose horses
wouldn't think to go.

I've wakened to their iron clatter
on the road, caught up
a neighbor's mare and searched
among the empty fields and dripping woods.
No sign of horses anywhere above
the sleeping town, although I've sensed
them close and watching me.

They come down toward afternoon,
ambling loose-hipped, uncontrite,
and always by some path I'd sought
them on. We've seen them heading home
from half a mile away, unhideable
as elephants against a yellow slope.

A state trooper dropped by this morning to say he'd be forced to arrest my ducks and me if I didn't start keeping them in a pen. He apologized and said he felt rather silly about the nature of the call, but that a neighbor had complained about them running loose. E. B. White once wrote a memorable line about how his chickens had taken to "whoring and singing," and if my nine Muscovies had been up to those shenanigans, I'd have dragged the law into the matter, too. But all they were doing, according to a tart little note from the lady down the street, was sitting on her porch railing quacking at passersby. That's a natural enough thing for a duck to do and I don't see the harm in it.

Nearly every morning, Billy Chase's sow comes by to play with the Arab, and it has never occurred to me to have her arrested. She's a jolly little pig, just brimming with *joie de vivre*. The two of them—the gray gelding and the dawn-colored sow—romp and cavort around the pasture like a pair of puppies. They're marvelous fun to watch. Billy told me the other day, though, that he'll probably have to confine her to a pen. She has taken to wandering all over Gilead, and he's afraid she'll forget to come home some night.

Last night I went down to the stable to check on the foal and put the turkey in his pen. Before I did, though, I sat on the floor and began chatting with him. He seems to like this, along with my scratching his hideous head, which changes from gray to a flamboyant red when he is stroked.

This time, however, he commenced bumping and crowding me. I let him, curious about what it would lead to. He next fastened on my extended leg—his grip was remarkably strong—and lowered himself over it, tail and wing tips pressing the floor. Then damned if he didn't start making love to it, pumping furiously away and panting in ecstasy. I was at a loss about what to do. How does one say no to a turkey, especially given that it is scheduled for imminent execution? Might it not be charitable to let this lonely fellow, last of the flock, have his way with me?

Yet how could I go at life past this point with the same innocence as before? Suppose it got serious? What terrible place in hell is reserved for those who have had an affair, however brief, with a turkey? How could I face my children, my colleagues, the teller at the drive-up window? A terrible shame crept up my left leg. I fancied I could hear the other one whisper to it, "You cheap slut!"

38

He didn't linger after the act. What's done is done. I only hope he won't go bragging to the goose and ducks.

Early this morning I noticed that the turkeys had found their way out of the door I'd left open and were in the barnyard, strutting and poking about. A half-hour later when I looked again, however, there was no sign of them anywhere, so I pulled on my boots and went hunting for them. Turkeys have no sense of destination, nor do they ever seem to develop a familiarity with their home grounds. They simply wander off and have to be fetched back. I have come across them hopelessly lost in the next door neighbor's yard and have also found them walking down the road toward town, apparently incapable of turning around.

There was no sign of them anywhere. A neighbor out walking, though, told me he'd just seen my birds. "Where?" I asked. "Watching the carpenters," he said.

So I walked what would amount to a city block down to where the big house on the corner is being renovated. One fellow was up on the roof ripping out shingles, and two more were on the ground working at a table saw. The birds were standing in the driveway spectating. I don't mean this fancifully; there is no more accurate way to describe what they were doing. If I had chosen to observe the goings-on, I would have been drawn to precisely the same spot, and my gaze would have fastened on the same activities that drew their attention. I stood watching them for a couple of minutes, noting that the carpenters' certain astonishment must have worn off, for they ignored the turkeys' presence and stuck to their work.

What struck me was the terribly human demeanor of the things. They did not seem even slightly incongruous standing there, but instead resembled two very white, plump passersby having nothing better to do than let themselves become engrossed as an alternative to boredom. They are normally a

39

raucous, agitated, and ungainly pair. Now, though, they had discovered a reticence that amounted almost to dignity. Their warty heads moved in perfect syncopation with the movements of the men; when a cast-off shingle spun from roof to ground, they solemnly watched its descent; although they will bark and gobble excitedly at any noise in the barn, they stood utterly still and silent in the bedlam of hammering, ripping, and sawing. "How long have they been standing here?" I asked the foreman. "About an hour," he said.

Herding these two toms from place to place is never a problem; they go where they are driven with a complacency one doesn't expect from such profoundly stupid foul. But when I attempted to guide them back to the yard, I had a dreadful time of it. Usually I start one with a push and he keeps on going in that same general direction. This time, however, they behaved like wretched children. The larger one especially was determined to continue watching the job. No matter how hard I pushed, he'd wheel away and trot back to his spot. When finally I took him by a wing, he locked his feet in place and refused to budge. It took fully fifteen minutes to drag him home, his protests filling the morning. The other followed but paused half a dozen times to look back at the job, the way a person will when he's reluctant to leave off watching something fascinating.

## FIRING ORDER

The firing order on a Ford 8-N
is 1-2-4-3. Earl knew it in
his sleep, the blue fire yearning in
the iron block, the smokepipe
counting out the sequence,
1-huff, 2-huff, 4-huff, 3.
Tyler'd had the cap off the distributor
for sure. Wanda said he was mechanical,
like Earl. He remembered when
he took apart the starter on
his father's Allis Chalmers how
Earl Senior whipped him with
his belt. You had to draw the line
somewhere.

When he shot the veal calf, he'd aimed
an inch too high. It shook its head
and bellowed, then broke free and
spun in circles til it finally dropped.
He'd made Tyler a part of it. You had to.
The boy had run off crying, and Wanda
wouldn't talk to him for days.
Now, near an hour of tinkering before
he'd noticed that the cables weren't
going where they should.

Combustion chambers were
like little worlds, and there was law
in there, an order to the way things had
to be, the pistons rushing up,
the whoosh of fire that drove
them down. It was too much to explain.
When Wanda shut the Hoover off,
he told her he was going to have
to give the boy a licking.

41

The forecast is for still more snow. The wind will carry it into the stable. It will dust the bedding and drift up the corridors, taking back to itself what long ago the barn's builder thought he had claimed for his own. The wind never ceases here in winter. It comes from the north, irresistible and unforgiving. It blows from the lakes, drinking up great draughts of icy water and turning liquid into stinging snow when it reaches the cold shores. There is a terrible logic to winters here; it pre-exists anything we humans know.

The horses understand, however. It is part of their design. Winter is a matter of patience, not resistance. They turn their tails to it; their thick, unruly coats hold in metabolic heat; their sharp hooves find forage; their perfect teeth tear it loose from the frozen ground.

This is what one thinks about mornings while forking up manure and breaking ice from water pails: the ancient intelligence of animals. No species is without thought; no animal is stupid. A horse looks stolid in a blow, a bulk of forlorn ignorance. But that is because they take the wind within the grain of their being; turning away from it is not surrender but acceptance. It lifts the ruff of their coats without penetrating; it forgets them. It is not that I love horses, although I do; it is that it is important to look closely at another form of life so that we can keep honed a sense of humility, and from that, perhaps, a wisdom.

## FIRST FROST

The first hard frost does more
than his small death. I'd have found
in spring a paradox about the killing of
a foal—some fit eulogy would come.
But the light is low and cold, the pale
hay rank and broken all around the hole
I dug. It whispered grief enough when
it flattened under him.

I climb the twisted path to pasture,
pick up the few hard pears that
have fallen past the fence, crush ·
between my fingers a rosary of nightshade,
curse just once. Nothing else. Hill
after hill the blowy sky and what
few pigeons leave the silo's dome.

I've just completed a very pleasant evening with a recipe
book compiled by Mrs. Delos Cummings. It's the first work
of its kind I've ever read through and probably the last, for
cooking is even less interesting to me than a High Mass said
in Latin. Mrs Cummings's volume, though, is only at first a
collection of recipes; beneath this matter of appearances is
what's engaging: something of the person who brought the
words together, and past that, something about life itself.

It may seem unlikely that in a cookbook much of its
author gets a chance to show. Here, however, even the
work's externals give hints about its compiler. The book
itself was never meant for recipes; it's one of those black-
covered spiral-bound appointment calendars that executives
consult before telling you they can't see you until next July.
The tops of its pages are decorated with such italicized head-

ings as "Residence Burglary and Theft Problems," and "Paymaster, Messenger and Interior Robbery Policies," and below them with ample space between are two days' worth of dates in boldface. Mrs. Cummings has written her recipes over, under, and around this officiousness, and when she has run short of room, the penciled instructions and ingredients climb whimsically up and down the margins.

I like the recipes' names too, and how the author has bothered to credit her sources. There are, for example, Mrs. Yocum's Very Good Lemon Pie, Mrs. Lincoln's Plain Mince Meat, Mina Host's Poor Man's Fruit Cake, Miss Dobbin's Boiled Salad Dressing, Mrs. Purtell's Good Cold Relish, Mrs. Churchill's Very Good Way To Cook a Pot Roast, Maggie's Molasses Cake, Beets for Dinner Any Day (again Mrs. Yocum), Amy Wilkson's Chunk Pickles, Mrs. Brown's Way with Carrots, Miss Urtell's Pickled Cherries, Anna's World War One Cake, Mrs. Egg Woman's How to Put Up Pickles, and Cake from Radio, 1946.

There's an upbeat, busy sound about some of these titles too: Ice Cream Number Two, Lightning Cake, Apple Dapple, Busters, and Emergency Pudding. But what I found most attractive among the entries in Mrs. Cummings's collection were those recipes that belong to the author herself and are by implication a legacy and a treasure. These—and there are many—bear the gently proud stamp "Mother's Way." Find me a prettier label for a recipe than Pick-a-Lily Mother's Way.

What keeps people other than devoted cooking hobbyists away from recipe collections is, I'm certain, their sterile and voiceless quality. You can't find anybody in them. But this author, like any good writer, keeps popping up in the text. Making pickles Amy Wilkson's way is, she comments parenthetically, "lots of work." About another dish she concludes playfully, "Fry it and try it." When you can corn Mrs. Brown's way, judgment counts: you either "let the milky water cover the corn or sort of cover it"; for Nora Kahn's

Pork Cake, you've got to "make the batter stiff but not too stiff," and to make Good Catsup, you begin with "as many tomatoes as you want." To put up pickles Mrs. Egg Woman's way, add "ten cents worth" of saccharine to a gallon of brine, or for a quart, "what will go on the end of a knife." "I always go by guess," she confesses in the middle of one recipe, but because it is Mother's Way to Make Sausage, I have no doubt that her guesses are unerring.

What shows in this collection is the exhausting work it was for a woman to keep her family fed in hard country. There are few prepared ingredients; nearly everything begins from scratch. There are warnings about the fire getting too hot, countless instructions to slice, skin, peel, dice, to drain or strain or simmer daily for long stretches. Winter wafts through the pages of Mrs. Cummings's little book, for many of the recipes deal with putting food by, with canning, curing, pickling. To cure hams, begin with a hog; for sausage, "take about seventy-five lbs. meat"; to pickle beef or pork you need a hundred pounds of either and eight pounds of salt.

In the initial instruction for Mother's Way to Make Head Cheese is implicitly what it meant to run a household here half a century ago: "First of all keep stirring all the while," and in its concluding line the certitude and satisfaction that all the toil in between will count for something: "It will keep nicely."

❧

SHOWER AT EVEN
*(Random Lines from the Diary of James H. Thomson, the Years 1838–1840)*

James Steele went past
with the sleigh and the bells,
the wind ahowling on the house
all smokey like Indian Summer.

The sap run fast, the rime
was white, the anchor ice remained.
John carried my Coat to Eri Grays
and old Sam Kinion come.

The Bees was out like summer,
another ewe had twins.
We threshed with the horses
and some with the Flails and I
drawed some Stones & dung.

We mowed in the head of the meddow
and the wind blows up
like a storm, the dampness is
aflying and it looks
some like a storm.

Bing told me the other night about an eighty-year-old woman who used to go to revival meetings at church. "When she let out a whoop and jumped over three pews, you could tell the spirit had hit her." It brought to mind my visit with B. Gage and his pretty, blue-eyed wife. The conversation swung back to early times, and he noted that when he first saw Gilead it was from the seat of a horse-drawn wagon. During the Depression, he said, "We was as poor as Job's turkey. Got so weak we had to lean up against the fence just to eat."

His wife started twitting him about how he'd spoiled their daughter. "I swear," she said, "if she'd have asked you for a lookin' glass and a hammer, you'd have handed them right over."

"Jumped-up Jesus" falls somewhere between interjection and expletive. I've never heard it used outside of town and have no idea what its etymology may be. Some folks here are known to be "tighter than the bark on a tree"; others are "too stupid to pour piss out of a boot." A milder form of insult is to be called "a side-hill ploughboy," the suggestion being that one leg has grown longer than the other to fit the contours of a hilly farm. For that matter, "side-hill" is the accepted term for "slope," a word one seldom hears in these parts. A dairy farmer "pulls tits" for a living, nor does one farm but instead "farms it," as in "I've been farming it for thirty years."

A "blind ditch" is a buried drainage canal filled with loose stone; a "barway" is an opening in a stone wall to admit farm vehicles. Here, though, it isn't a stone wall but a "stone wall fence." For loggers, "roadside" functions as a verb, as in "I roadsided three cord today" (drew pulpwood out to the road to be picked up by trucks from the mill). To prepare yourself for such killing work, it's best to begin with a hearty breakfast, say three or four eggs and a stack of "pannycakes" (which are often served with white gravy rather than syrup).

I discovered last winter that what I used to skim down snowy hills with isn't a sled but a hand sleigh. Always in this country of harsh winters, you'd better have your outside chores completed "before the snow flies," which includes splitting firewood so you'll have enough "sticks" (never logs) to see you through. You don't, of course, waste your time on "dozy" (rotten) wood. The tool most of us use for splitting is a "go-devil," an axe-like implement with a wide-flaring head.

Although the terms are in common use beyond this valley, most Americans don't know how much wood there is in a cord, and even fewer understand the difference between that standard of measurement and a face cord. The former amounts to a stack of logs sawn into four-foot lengths and measuring eight feet long and four feet high. The latter is as long and as high as a full cord, but the logs have been cut to stove length, approximately sixteen inches. Thus, it takes three face cords to make a full cord.

This morning I asked Bobby about another term I'd heard him use as an apparent measure of firewood. "How much wood's in a jag?" I said.

"What do you mean 'how much?'"

"I mean is a jag like a cord, so long, so high?" I asked.

"Jag's anything you want it to be; don't make any difference," he explained.

"What kind of answer is that?" I said. "You tell me you're going up to the woodlot to draw out a jag, and I'm not supposed to be surprised if you come back with a load of rocks?"

"That ain't what I meant. A jag's just a jag, that's all. Truck, wagon, don't matter what size it is; it's whatever you decide to throw on."

"You mean if I asked you to sell me half a jag of wood, you couldn't do it?"

"Course I could."

"Well, all right," I said. "What would I get?"

"Screwed good," he said.

🐜

PARTS OF SPEECH

Take me where no mawling is,
O Lord, where winnowing is like
To be. Guide me ever in
Your harrow, and I will cast
Go-devils down and ted
Long windrows in your name.

The shining disk of you!
How bright against the chaff and bale,
The boar and sow of everyday.

I lay up stone in hope
That barways open
Unto you, that hame
And whiffle-tree are shoat
Enough.

Hear my Alfalfas, Lord,
The yield and second cutting
Of my love.

Up here auctions are a source of recreation just as much as places to pick up bargains. I had to be dragged to my first one, in a drafty, steel-sided barn. By the end of the evening I'd acquired a chair with a busted-out wicker seat, an inoperative chainsaw, and an orange tomcat that I hadn't bid on but that the auctioneer said he'd drown if nobody took it.

These things grow on a person. It got so Friday nights the auctioneer gave me a wave and a smile, knowing I was probably going to sit on my hands all evening but that I admired the way he ran his show and that I'd laugh at all his jokes. He was a master auctioneer, cannily reading his audience, sensing in advance who'd buy what and for how much, cajoling the reluctant and exploiting the gullible, throwing together odd lots of unsaleable junk into irresistible packages, accepting opening bids from nonexistent bidders. I came to love those Friday nights. Always I ended up spending five dollars on something, as a way of paying admission.

Sometimes when I was in the barn or off in the truck, I'd play at being an auctioneer, but I never got it right—the lightning-fast sing-song babble, I mean, those inchoate syllables spilling forth that reminded me of Sid Caesar pretending to be Italian. I can't even write out a fair imitation of that mechanical patter. And yet it's a language, with its own unique inflections and grammar, and you can hear it spoken in auction barns throughout this region and, I discovered, in countless other rural regions too. There are schools for it. My auctioneer attended one in Kentucky, a two-week course in which, among other things, he learned the hypnotic spiel of his trade. I asked him one night what it was for, and he said simply, "To keep things moving." Silence in an auction barn is unnatural enough to be ominous, eerie.

But I just as much enjoyed another form of dialect, this one more immediately local. Invariably, a chest or bureau was described as having "three [or four, etc.] drawers *into* it"; TV's that lit up but produced no sound or picture were "hummers" (analogously, at livestock auctions aged horses are described as being "smooth of tooth"); teeth on a wood-saw were typically "fine as frog hair"; and more than once I heard a broken-down piece of furniture depicted as "nothing you couldn't fix with an axe." Instead of kitchen chairs or tractor tires or buzz saw blades being auctioned off individually, they were thrown together in lots and sold "all for one money," another way to keep things moving. Toward the end, the detritus of the evening was randomly dumped into cartons and auctioned as "boxes of contents," so oxymoronic a phrase I've never been able to quite work it out.

Some people hold that auctions, these little weekly ones at least, are no more than a form of refuse disposal, and that auctioneers are predators who feed on the hopes of the poor and ignorant. That may be true of the operations that gypsy around the country selling junk power tools, but it doesn't fit most local enterprises. True, you're stuck with that you buy (although more than once I've turned back an item that upon close inspection proved to be defective). And yes, most of the items that come up for bid would otherwise have been trashed by their owners. Indeed, furniture is often splattered with pigeon droppings acquired from sitting years in a barn. But patrons are always encouraged to come early and look over the merchandise. Furthermore, most auctioneers are fairly scrupulous about describing flaws, even though they may minimize them: "Little chip off the edge here. Just keep it turned toward the wall." "We had her running out back this afternoon. Needs a set of plugs is all." And never have I seen a local auctioneer badger those who come just to spectate.

I've bought my share of junk at these affairs, including boxes of contents, but I've also come away with gems, including a drawknife I wouldn't trade for gold, a lovely handmade quilting rocker, and the corn chopper that sits ten feet from me, unselfconsciously elegant and with a patina acquired over decades of use. Altogether, they cost about thirty dollars. As for honesty, I once bought a wicker chaise and couldn't fit it in the car. So I left it at the auction barn, promising to pick it up early the next week. I never bothered, however; the piece wasn't worth the trip. A month later I received a check in the mail. The auction had re-sold it, and I'd made six dollars on the deal.

## DOMBROSKI'S BULL

Earl lit his breakfast cigarette
and thought on how to kill
the Polack's bull, which took him
back through everything he knew
about the Poles in general, which
was nothing much except they seemed
to run on cabbage.

No sooner had he got the Jimmy on
the road again the night before
and was coming down from Butch's place
the back way in and slowing for the dip
than a rushing slab of something blacker
than the ink-black end of everything
came tearing through a hedgerow and gored
him in the grille. Earl didn't even have a name
at first for what he thought had got him
til it ran up the Polack's porch and he
could see it by the mercury light. It was
the worst ten seconds in his life since
something grabbed him by the toe when he
was swimming in the creek.

So he said to Wanda that the first dark night
he'd shoot Dombroski's bull because
you couldn't kill it with a truck, he'd tried
that twice and it had come to most
of a front end, three headlights and a jug
of muscatel. She shook her head and said
she didn't know him anymore and which
way did he want his eggs.

General stores are not so much businesses as palpable man-
ifestations of their proprietors' natures. There are those
establishments with a meanness about them. Chill and dark
even in summer, their shelves mostly empty, they personify a
falling out with life, a cheerless fatalism about what tomorrow will bring. One never lingers long in these places, for
they weigh down the heart. Yet there are just as many little
enterprises that advertise the opposite—that say, despite lean
times or howling winters, all is well, the earth will bloom
again, there is reason to be glad.

52

Our general store is such a place. It is warm and bright, and on its shelves one can find—

eyebolts, stove bolts, U-bolts and carriage bolts;
birdfood, catfood, dogfood, and fishfood;
birthday cards, Christmas cards, Easter and condolence cards;
rubbers, galoshes, barn boots, and Gorilla-brand workshoes;
kite string, ribbon, rope, and chain;
contraceptives, envelopes, liver pills, and handkerchiefs;
Copenhagen , O.B. Joyful, Red Man, and plug;
shotgun shells, deer slugs, .22s and thirty-ought-sixes;
inner tubes, long underwear, hair spray, and dental floss;
wallets, purses, Big Ben clocks, and pantyhose;
jackknives, boning knives, steak knives, and skinning knives;
fishhooks, lures, lines, and nets;
rocksalt, potting soil, pie tins, and Aspergum;
coveralls, sparkplugs, pump leathers, and teething rings;
Jujubes, licorice whips, gumdrops, and Tootsie Rolls;
heating pads, hot water bottles, Posted signs, and valve cores;
beads, brooches, bracelets, and three kinds of suspenders;
notebooks, pencils, pens, and erasers;
brush saws, pliers, drill bits, and hammers;
smoke pipe, septic pipe, copper pipe, and pipe cleaners;
fennel, dill, anise, and cinnamon;
flux, solder, welding rod, and rivets.

I'm just skimming; there's much, much more, including bag balm and cow magnets. These two items deserve special comment: the former, also referred to as udder balm, comes in pretty, grass-green tins decorated with five red clover blossoms. According to its makers, bag balm is meant to cure "chapped teats and superficial scratches." This, however, is a starkly modest claim, for bag balm will cure nearly anything. Nothing I know will touch it as an emollient and healing agent. If I could reach down into my often-blistered soul, I would smear it liberally with the stuff and know that within an hour or so things would be right again. We have used it on cuts, burns, infections—both human and equine—and it has never failed us. One fellow here in town swears he rubs it on his hangovers, and I know him for an honest man.

Cow magnets are useful in other ways. They are cylindrical devices, rounded at the ends and about an inch in diameter and half again as long. As I understand it, you drop them into cows and they lodge in the cecum and pick up stray little bits of metal that bovines somehow ingest while grazing. Unlike bag balm, cow magnets won't work with humans, or at least I don't know of anyone who has bothered to swallow one. Still, they have a use beyond what their manufacturer envisioned, for I have never discovered any man-made object more wonderful to tell lies about. If, for example, you have lost your herd, all you have to do is leave one of these things in the field, and cows from all over the county will collect around it in minutes. Or there was the farmer from the next town who put a metal roof on his barn and came out in the morning to find all his milkers hanging from the ceiling. The possibilities are endless; in the lowly cow magnet lives more good lies than have been spawned by the Bermuda Triangle or the White House.

The inventory I listed doesn't include groceries and might have led you to think that the place is a department store. Not so; you can buy nearly any kind of basic food, including fresh meat and vegetables on most days. Furthermore, you can buy them without paying anything. What you do is say, "Put it on my bill," and when you remember, maybe a month later, you say, "Here's twenty dollars," or if you're flush, you pay it off. There's a forlorn little hand-lettered sign taped to the cash register that warns about carrying charges for overdue accounts, but it is, I'm nearly certain, an empty threat. Our storekeeper puts in about seventy hours a week in the place, and I figure he's too bushed at night to go home and peck away at his calculator trying to arrive at such assessments. Furthermore, he's too goodnatured. Never once have I received a bill, and he has carried me through some long, desperate stretches. He would extend credit to a dog if he knew one of its parents.

There is no cracker barrel or potbellied stove in the store, but it is hands down the coziest, most congenial spot in town to loiter, as well as being a wonderful classroom. Once, to research an article on dialect, I spent the entire day there, grilling long-time residents about odd or pretty-sounding terms I'd been jotting down over the years. It was a fascinating experience; no amount of digging through books would have yielded up as much. But more, it is the one place in town to which everyone sooner or later comes, and a hundred times at least I've struck up conversations that would not have happened elsewhere and learned a thousand things I hadn't known before. It was a memorable delight to meet the good-looking, whip-thin old gentleman who explained to me how he trained mules for the Army back in World War I, or to learn from Inez, as I did last spring, that she is glad she got out of school fifty years before my kind took them over.

Toward evening old cronies drift in. It is what passes here for cocktail hour, and because our host is, to quote Emerson, "good company for pirates and good with academicians," nearly anyone is welcome. There are proprieties: during store hours it is illegal to drink within the place, and so we stand behind the long meat cooler toward the back and hold our beer cans low. It's only a ritualized gesture. No one who has lived here for more than a week is fooled into thinking that the half-dozen fellows back there are crouching down to inspect the salami.

## CLAYTON BLOOM

Clayton Bloom came mornings up
our only street, red Bruno pulling him.
The dog, like Clayton's coat, was oversize,
a bear, its ruff-cowled anvil of
a skull concluding in a leer.

Clayton's daily habit was to pause
a dozen times to argue with the wind
or chat with people no one else could see.
But Bruno's was to churn at flank-
speed to the store, his master jerking like
an empty skiff behind. And so
their journey seemed a metaphor,
with Clayton's hanging back what anyone
would finally do.

The red dog always wins, of course.
Some unrelenting malady dragged Clayton in
his flapping coat to death, who didn't know
his age or how to read a clock and told
me once that doctors had removed
his heart when he was still a boy.
Which makes me wonder if perhaps
he went less vexed and terrified
than others on the hill.

A month ago my friend Conrad called to say that he planned
to reconnoiter a big league cock fight not far from here. He
assumed that I'd be interested in attending. For the two
weeks preceding the event I prayed for a severe cold or that
he'd get arrested again. But he appeared last Saturday,
accompanied by Johnny, who only a couple of months

56

before had talked the sheriff out of locking him up by explaining that he, along with the dozen others who had fled out a back door, had gathered at midnight in a deserted barn with fifty or so cocks to conduct a chicken show.

It was zero degrees when we left for the affair. A fellow fancier had volunteered to guide us to the place from midpoint. Instead of warming us on our arrival, however, he dragged us to his garage to inspect at close hand his own assortment of birds. For forty minutes we stomped around out there, ducking vagrant pigeons and absorbing his theories on breeding, all of which were arcane and tainted with voodoo. He was, nevertheless, a committed kind of fool. He insisted that we now accompany him to a friend's place to look at still more birds. So we rocketed thirty miles southward to Long Eddy. I was put into the back seat with a surly rooster in a metal crate, which managed to work its head out far enough to bite me on the leg.

In fairness, they were indeed tough birds that we visited with. Lesser creatures couldn't have survived in such a setting. The flock perched alternately on a forty-year-old bulldozer and a dead Holstein lying in the middle of the barn floor. The cow was quite frozen and will probably remain so until sometime in July, for the barn was nestled into the dark side of a hill and had no windows.

When at last my companions had satisfied themselves about the mettle of these cocks, their owner invited us in. On his porch I noticed a vividly dead rabbit that had been thrust headfirst into a plastic bucket. Our host noted that it had been dropped off by a friend but had been overlooked until, by now, "It would take a goddam buzz saw to gut it."

He was the nearly perfect host. The place was a hovel, but he quickly tidied up by plunging a mop into the toilet bowl in the kitchen and swishing it around the plywood floor. Next he placed one of his many small children on the table and changed her diaper, then served us coffee. I put mine aside to cool just long enough for one of two enormous

Plott hounds to run her long brown tongue into the depths of my cup. By that time, however, niceties no longer mattered; we shared what hadn't been spilled. The four of us then sped to the scene of the fight, a concrete-block building warmed only by the fervor of about eighty fools.

The prohibition against cock fighting is thought by the uninitiated to be woven into the general concern about cruelty to animals. This is a misguided notion. Game cocks are bred to frenzy; they are good for nothing other than battle. It is impossible to know them for their charm, intelligence, or sensitivity. They are stupid, mean corruptions of God's better intentions and wake not wanting breakfast but something resembling themselves to kill. Cock fighting was outlawed because of its demoralizing effect on the audience. The most acutely sympathetic conscience reduces after the third or fourth bout to the state of ennui, from there proceeds to desperate boredom, and thus inevitably to a rancid stupefaction. I am an avowed animal lover. Within a half-hour I was muttering "Die, so the next bird can die and I can extricate my frozen backside from this calamity."

We got out of there at about midnight, the temperature by then having dropped to twenty below. I doubt I have ever been so desperately miserable. Conrad and Johnny, however, were so taken by the night's business that the cold seemed not to bother them at all. Considerable money had been wagered over the evening—I'd guess a couple thousand at least—and the two of them went on about which of their birds could have cleaned up against the night's contestants. "Hell," Conrad said, "I got a couple of stags would've wiped out anything I saw tonight." (A stag is a young cock still in training, somewhere between egg and Charles Manson.) And Johnny averred that he had a hen he'd pit against half the cocks on the program. They'd won about ten thousand dollars apiece by the time they dropped me off, numb and dispirited, in front of the house.

(Last fall Conrad invited me in the middle of a midnight thunderstorm to help him find an illegal deer he'd shot. We walked almost straight up in the lashing rain, ducking spectral alders and falling into black ditches. We came upon the deer, a small buck, after trekking a couple of miles in inky darkness. There was no way to get him out save dragging, so I volunteered my belt, hooking it about the short antlers. The drag was mostly downhill and easy enough until my pants dropped, propelling both of us into a long, drenching slide down a steep slope and badly raking my buttocks. The buck and I ended up in a water-filled culvert half a mile from the truck. Despite what I may have told you toward the first, there is precious little tranquility to be found in the country. You're better off by far lounging on streetcorners waiting for walk lights.)

### PITTING STAGS

Earl thought Nipper maybe had
a chance against the bronzy red
that Olin bragged about, or why
come all this way, a tire soft
and Tyler in the back asleep.
Just stags they were. He would
have swung south onto Shale Bank
but for the leaky tire.

He'd blow across the young bird's
yellow eyes, across his clipped-
off comb, whisper "Get 'm, boy,"
and put him in the pit. It didn't win
you any money, pitting stags.
He turned the radio to KTY,
then shut it off.

All week long he'd seen things
a person doesn't want to see.
His father'd cut his thumb half off
buzzing firewood; up in Egypt poachers
hung ten deer in Plevin's barn
then must've lost their nerve.
He'd found them, three months dead
and rotting in their nooses.
Four cocks killed at Olin's Friday night,
which put him down to two,
not counting half a dozen stags.

Nipper had the size, the legs, the night
was full of stars. He checked that Tyler
was asleep, took just a little drink,
and turned the radio back on.

Yesterday just past noon the largest of three towering poplar trees at the edge of the yard blew over and broke our house's back, tore off the front porch, smashed windows, took out the power and telephone lines, and laid general waste to the place. The small tornado that caused the havoc was aimed directly at me; the only additional local damage was to a shed up the road, if one doesn't count all the other trees that came down unerringly on nothing. When God spoke from the whirlwind yesterday afternoon, I couldn't catch His exact words over the rest of the racket, but the message was easy enough to figure out: something about me sticks in His craw.

Unless you go around to the back door, the only way into the place presents an interesting kind of challenge. You've got to hitch yourself up on a tree trunk out by the road and balance your way across the yard, with the trunk inclining upward until by the time you reach what's left of the front door you're maybe five feet off the ground. Then you jump down through some branches into the livingroom. I may leave it that way just for the novelty of it and to keep off the idly curious. To get in here now you've got to be sober and athletic, and most people I know aren't up to being both at the same time.

I wasn't arguing above, by the way, that there isn't any rightness to the Lord's wrath. I'd sooner think that yesterday's calamity proved just the opposite. It doesn't take that much wisdom to conclude that if this were a simple case of Divine whimsy, He could as soon have dropped an oak tree on the place instead of just an eight- or nine-ton poplar. Furthermore, it was clear that I was getting still another chance. We figured the tractor up in the woodlot was probably smashed to bits, but what the storm had done was skip over our section and come down half a mile farther in, where it uprooted about five acres of the tallest, straightest red pines anywhere on state land. So Tom and I rushed straight over to the conservation office and bought enough of them to build a cabin. I'll start skidding them out next week. With any luck we'll be in the place before the snow flies. The Lord giveth, the Lord taketh away. And vice-versa.

CATTLE CROSSING

"Can't you hurry them a bit?"
I shouted at the boy
who'd strung a herd of fifty cows
across my way.

"Won't do no good," he said.
"You push them and they scatter."

To weight his answer with reproof,
a cow the color of a domino
turned out from all the rest
and shook her hornless head at me.

I took it for admonishment,
at least, the gist of which
I'd learned a hundred hilly roads ago:
That men and cows have long agreed
on where and when to meet,
and this flat crossing place and hour
are all that's congruous between the two.

Keep me from my commerce, then.
Come milking time the way belongs to you.

A year ago this month Grover stopped by on a Saturday afternoon looking extra tense. He'd come around to the back door, which isn't his usual way, and said right off, "You want to buy a gun?"

I didn't know which gun he meant; he had a raft of them. I wasn't interested in acquiring another gun anyhow. I had a couple of shotguns that had sat propped and unused in a closet for years and a single-action .22 magnum hidden away in the crawl space that I'd been planning to give Grover just to get rid of it. But I was interested in what inspired the offer, so I said, "Maybe. Which one do you mean?"

"My .357," he said. "The one Harriet give me for Christmas." Now I knew there was a story behind his coming by. That revolver was his pride and joy. He'd only had it for about two months, but he had mentioned long before that how he lusted to own it ever since he'd spotted it on display at the hardware store. He pulled it out of his coat, placed it on the table, and undid the dish towel it was wrapped in.

"Half-price," he said, "and she's practically brandnew." It was a mean-looking weapon. I didn't even want to be in the same room with such a cannon, with its over-size walnut grips, its gleaming nickel finish, its bore big enough for a rat to run up. "You ever fire it?" I asked him, and he said yes, about a half-hour ago.

"Nearly shot my mother-in-law," he added. He'd taken it out of the drawer to show it off to her, he explained, and when he went to demonstrate how you pull the hammer back to cock it, his thumb had slipped. "Blew a helluva big hole in the kitchen wall right over her head. Jesus, Peter, you should have seen the size of the flame that come out of the barrel!"

I asked him how his mother-in-law had felt about the incident, and he said what seemed to upset her most was the plaster getting into her hair and down the back of her blouse. Apparently there had been a conference of sorts just seconds later among Grover, Harriet, and his in-laws, the gist of which was that life is chancy enough without his shooting holes in the house with a Christmas present. "I hate to sell her," he said, "but she's just too damn slippery for me."

I wasn't even tempted; no one needs a howitzer like that. But I ended up shooting it a few months later on a Saturday afternoon when there was a pleasant little crap game going on in Grover's kitchen with him and Johnny and his girlfriend Trudy, and we took a break and went out back to shoot holes in a bucket. That .357 kicked so bad a person couldn't hit a mother-in-law with it from six feet away. My brother dropped by from Connecticut about then, and the first thing he asked was what with the crap game and guns going off in the backyard was there anything legal at all about this town. Grover told him hell yes, that there was a brandnew sticker on the gas pump down at the store from the Bureau of Weights and Measures.

🐜

Bill Ortmann lives in shabby circumstances with his wife Irene and their two retarded daughters, Bebe and Ramona. Bill's about eighty and has terrible vision and a hearing problem. (He and Irene snack regularly on milk of magnesia poured on saltines, which is what is called here a "true fact.")

Bobby told me last week that the Ortmanns have the meanest patch of horseradish in town, so when I spotted Bill down at the air pump outside the store, I decided to ask him if I could dig some. He was inflating a tire, with Bebe watching. I tapped him on the back a couple of times and Bebe said, "He don't hear too good."

"I didn't say anything yet," I said. I tapped him again, this time pretty hard, and he hitched up from his crouch and blinked at me through miles-deep lenses. I know Bill fairly well, but he doesn't know anyone who's moved to town since his eyes gave out. "Hello Bill," I said. "How you been?"

His mouth opened slowly and worked at saying something but stopped. Bebe said, "He don't hear you." The air hose dangled from his hand, emitting random dings. It was inflating all of Gilead.

"Say, Bill," I started, "Bobby says you've got a patch of horseradish you might want to get rooted up. Okay if I dig some?" His gaze wavered. He looked down at the tire in a thoughtful way, then over at Bebe, then finally back at me.

"Didn't getcha," he said.

I cranked up. "BILL," I shouted, "Bobby Shafer said you had some HORSERADISH. I want it, OKAY?"

"He don't hear you," Bebe pointed out.

"Can't hear ya," Bill said, cupping his hand to his ear.

"You say somethin' about a horse?"

"Bobby . . . Bobby Shafer!" I bellowed. "Horse-RADISH!"

Bill leaned toward me, squinting hard to catch whatever vague image I presented. "Shafer don't have no horserad-ish," he shouted back. "Wants some of ours."

I looked over at fat Bebe, who was wearing a sly grin. "You gotta talk louder," she said. "He don't hear good at all."

Bill was squatting down with his tire again, having lost all interest in me. "Slow leak," he muttered to himself. I bent over next to him, my mouth no more than six inches from his right ear: "I WANT YOUR HORSERADISH . . . I WANT TO DIG UP YOUR HORSERADISH. OKAY?"

Bill reared up in alarm, staring wildly at me as if he had been unaware until that minute that he wasn't entirely alone on the planet. "Good God, man, y' scared the bejeesus outta me!"

I opened my mouth to apologize, but he cut me off by shouting over my shoulder at his daughter, who was stand-ing maybe fifteen feet away. "What's he want, Beeb?"

"Wants to know if he can dig up some horseradish," she told him.

"Oh," he responded and turned back to the tire.

Then Bebe said to me, "We don't have no more horse-radish anyway. Wayne Freeman come by last week and dug it all up."

## THE GIRL WHO SMELLS LIKE HORSES

The girl who smells like horses
comes to firehouse dances
Friday nights. I don't agree
with those who say she
doesn't care enough about herself
to scrub the smell away.
(Half of her accusers reek of
cattle dung themselves.)

Her scent is nothing like a beast's
trapped stinking in a stall,
but close to being horse itself,
as if she met her Morgan
far from any barn, and lay
along his broad brown back,
and pressed her face among
the blue-black strands of mane.

You can gladly dance with such a smell,
and think of big, swinging necks,
and how a horse's snort blows flat
the morning grass.

I went this morning down to Bobby's to get back the chain
he borrowed a couple of years ago. I found him and Eddy in
the barn, each with a six-pack of Budweiser. It was cold
enough out there to hang meat, so I wondered aloud why
they'd chosen to roost in the shadows amidst the frigid iron
miscellany of the place, and Eddy said they were watching a
battery charge up and would I help them because they were
worn down to just about nothing from the chore. You can't
abandon good men in such circumstances; it goes against

some dim but urgent ethic. So I went across the road to the store and bought another six-pack, and the three of us sat there telling lies 'til nearly noon.

There is a peril to Saturday mornings here. I've not seen its like anywhere else. It is nearly impossible to stick to honest, boring work in a town peopled with Tom Sawyers, grown men who retain a boyish ability to disguise frivolity in the dress of high purpose. On a Saturday morning last fall I looked up from fixing a leaky faucet to spot Grover and Bobby stealing my apples. "We figured we'd make a little cider," Grover said, "to raffle at the dance." He told me they were going to borrow just a few more apples down the road and that maybe I should come along, inasmuch as I was dance chairman.

So of course I did, and over that long and unlikely autumn afternoon our piracies grew bolder, the quest for apples swinging out beyond a morning's whim into something grander, something that makes right the theft of fruit, the foolhardy climbing to the tops of old, brittle trees, even our finally charging the two trucks through the dense thicket that hems a meadow and its lone winesap up on Caskey Mountain.

I suppose it amounts to the ancient, unthought urge to pick before a wind blows down the fruit or the cold turns good apples into useless mush. Somewhere in our circuitry still lives a primal fear of winter, and the shaking down of apples is in the hope that we will live to see another spring. I'd forgotten that for a few millenia, and probably so had Grover and Bobby and the half-dozen others who'd attached themselves to our party as it wove its unsteady way across the yellowing middle of October. Perhaps, too, there's something in the nature of an apple beyond its homely usefulness that compels gluttony—the ruby glow when you buff one on your sleeve, or how in their tart taste are old, good memories—but now it was nearly night and we were stuck with our heaped and mostly useless spoils.

We stood there under that big old tree in the clearing and finished our beer. The pick-ups were filled to overflowing. I'd never seen so many apples in my life, and I remember feeling sheepish about its maybe having been just a silly game after all—that I'd run off gladly from a Saturday's chores still again to prank around the hills with my cronies.

Then Bobby said, " Killenberger's got that big press," so we rounded up every empty gallon jug in town and borrowed Gary Ball's whiskey barrel and rousted Billy Killenberger out of bed. It came to eighty-three gallons by the time we finished up two hours later. We drank cider all winter long, more eagerly as it took on a bit of effervescence the way cider will if you let it alone long enough. Some of it got to the dance, of course, along with one of my hens that Bobby borrowed to raffle off.

## EARL GETS CAUGHT

If there is anything about a widow,
it's that they'll draw an Earl
as if they sprayed the scent of need upon
the wind, the way a mare
does, and this one, eight miles up
the road and plump, hadn't been
bereaved for more than a few hours—
Del's indifferent heart had quit
the day a hemlock fell on him—
when Earl showed up and volunteered
to help her through her grief.
But Gloriann, who took in sewing
on the side, didn't take in Earl.

No then. It wouldn't have been right.
She waited two weeks past the funeral,
then said yes in the equipment shed
as many times as Molly Bloom, among
the chainsaws and the linchpins and
the unspooled cables of desire. A widow has
to get it someplace, she told her sister
from Dorloo. It helps keep off the change.
And it seemed safe enough, Earl's wife
her second cousin once removed, so it
would figure he would be the one to drop
by nights and bank her fire.

But Wanda was no fool. A month of Earl's
attentions to her cousin's woodstove and
she struck, or rather asked her little brother
Lauren Henry to, who stuffed a three-foot blacksnake
in the glove box next to Earl's half-pint of Gilbey's
while the Dodge was parked at Gloriann's.
It was nearly dawn when Earl showed up at home
on foot. He said to Wanda that the car had lost
a tie rod south of Good Luck Farm and bounded off
the road and thrown itself in Willy's pond.
That should have done it but it didn't.
According to Lucille down at the superette,
somebody'd seen the two of them the afternoon
before crawling out the silo chute up on
what used to be the Morgan place. And she
said she wasn't sure, but it had looked
like Earl's feet sticking out from under Del's
John Deere a week ago, and if they weren't,
why would the county pick-up truck he drove
be parked behind a hedge-row half a mile up
the road? "I'd mind my business,"
Lucille said, "but I think we got another
Pearl Macdougal on our hands."

So Wanda borrowed Earl's young sow
and painted "Gloriann" across her broad
pink flanks and turned her loose.
Earl had had to chase the thing from yard
to yard and up and down the road the better part
of Saturday, and anybody who could read
had read that low-slung billboard of a pig
and telephoned a neighbor to be sure
to watch the two of them go loping by.

That should have done it and it did.

Again I realize with uncharacteristic clarity how beautiful is the world, how achingly lovely this still-remote valley and the hills that shape it. On earth there cannot be a finer place. I'm not taken by it as are the occasional tourists who drive through and pause to snap busily away at autumn foliage or fields deep in pristine snow. There's that too—the panoramic prettiness of the Catskills. But what I sense early on this June morning is too private to yield to a blank-eyed camera or the stranger who aims it. I stand alone in a spruce lot and listen to the wind find a melody in the slender stiff limbs close to earth. (I'm not romanticizing; it's a very pretty sound.) Not far from where I'm standing—down a steep, overgrown path—is an ancient shale foundation. All around it is a wilderness of tag alders and raspberry bushes, and casting the place in shifting, flowing shadow, the ranked and towering red pines.

Whoever lived here took great pains about laying up stone. Enclosing the dooryard is a still-straight shale wall cut at intervals by wide stone stairs, more in keeping with a formal garden than a little span of yard. The spring is just as meticulously walled. I drank from it yesterday. Three maples line its upper edge, and the water is marvelously clear and cold. He, this nameless stranger from another century, built a splendid stone bridge across the stream. It's arched and in the middle of nothing faintly elegant and broad enough for a wagon to cross. On the far side is no sign of a road, just more pressing wilderness.

I sat on a log and studied his work for nearly an hour, wondering mostly about the fellow who'd chosen this unlikely hollow and where he'd found in him the strength and artistry and will to fit all these cold stones into such enduring symmetries; and why, too, he didn't follow the simpler way along the ridge rather than through this deep place and across its steep flank.

Then I climbed back up the path and near the top saw a great, brown-flecked hawk high in an oak tree and heard Dan's saw start up and then Tom's chime in right behind it, and soon the three of us were going at it, the big, stiff spruce falling in thumping dignity and the rain of needles and the smoke and rattle of the saws filling the woods. Later, when the day's work was done, we climbed a tall maple at the edge of a clearing and looked off into the distance at cow-peppered hills, and I noted to myself that the gray bark smells exactly the way it did when I was six.

We drove down the mountain and I stopped the truck at Gilead Creek. A mill stood there once; one of its walls forms part of the bridge. The pasture just above it was a pond then, but now the stream winds along its far edge, then down a series of dainty-stepped falls, and flows twisting and rushing into the woods. On spring nights, we can hear its drumming throb through the walls of the house. My sons are meant, I suppose, to move from here into a bigger world far from this place, but I dare to hope they'll sense that this is finally what they must come back to, where they truly belong.

CROSS TIES

The stallion stands in ties,
black against Sunday, the morning
slate and shaken with new wind,
sleet rattling on the stable roof.

Outside a willow shines in ice,
the neighbor's smoke runs low
across his yard. Suddenly I am
too old to love black horses.

It is another thing to seek, back
past reason into blood. A son stands
at the stallion's head. I wonder if
he senses I have come this far afraid.

I tell him that I led the colt
out in the night, but not that
when it reared and struck, I let
go the line and ran.

When you are old, I want to say,
some stallion will pull hard
enough against its chain to yank
the love of horses from your heart.
One afternoon up in the hills
I jumped a high stone wall aboard
his crazy roan. I want to say,
remember all of me for that. Remember
how we used to gallop bareback
almost up the sky.

# III

# THE MOUNTAIN

## WORD AND ICE

Winter's colder than its name.
Word and ice diverge.
What will say the frozen rut
of it, the chill enough
to rive a rock?

Or even April's bloom and swell.
What syllable lies sleeping in
a pod? stirs and rattles, shoots to green?

Too heavy-boned is any phrase
for all that shuttles, flutters, flings.
Nor will the slow names I have learned
catch minnow shine or swallows' wings.

The buck at the edge of the woods reacts to my scent. His head snaps up from cropping the long grass, the big eyes look at the wind, the nostrils flare, the long, erect ears rotate to the front. The layered muscles of his hindquarters bunch and twitch, a forefoot rises slightly, the jaws cease suddenly their incessant lateral movement. Through the binoculars I can see the long hairs on his underthroat stand out. Then he is gone in a single, noiseless bound, the big white tail as erect as fright itself.

Outside I hear the spring surging over flatnesses of gray stone and through the loamy channel it has dug. The northwest breeze always as now makes the huge old hemlock sough among its high green branches and rattle its brittle ones closer to earth.

A killdeer darts in nervous, narrow-winged flight above the haylot's ridge, like swift pen strokes on white, blank paper, and beyond, only endless mountain sky empty of clouds. The young hay, knee-high, is just now agreeably begun with daisies and is footed along the narrow road between my land and the hay's with floppy, Sunday-hat cowslips.

Yesterday I say on my wobbly picnic bench atop my grizzled mountain and spoke aloud and stirringly William Faulkner's Nobel Prize acceptance speech. The hemlocks listened, and so did three swallows. When I had done, the great attentive trees sighed and the birds left their apple bough and went darting and soaring prettily up my small piece of sky. The writer's business, I had told them, is to uplift man's heart, and I think they took our words, Bill's and mine, as high as wordladen swallows can fly and released them. I hope they hang there always, chiming on the wind, uplifting anyone who happens to pass beneath.

FROM HALF A FIELD AWAY

I hadn't seen the crouching hawk,
and when at first it made
to rise, it seemed a shaman's trick,
a mottled piece of pasture lured
to life. Beneath it swung
a wriggling silhouette of snake.

To reach its woods, the bird
would have to climb above the dished
field's rim and cross the road
where I had stopped to watch.
Storm-cloud shadow first it came,
neared the wilder height it sought....

My car astonished it.
There wasn't air enough for veer or lift.
The tawny rudders of its wings
convulsed, the beating shadow
covered me. Some cold and coiling
chemical crushed flat my lungs.

From half a field away
and at this early, misted hour,
I'd read into a predator and
prey a savage equilibrium.
But close, all balance broke
to glint of serpent shine,
blue talons sunk in belly plates,
two pairs of certain, stony eyes.

I'm bounded in by beauty. It even seeks me out in sleep. The other morning at about four I wakened to a racket just beneath me in the kitchen. A rat, I thought, and it's into the cake I bought at the school bake sale. I grabbed the flashlight and crept across the loft floor, more curious than determined. Hanging head and shoulders over the edge, I played the beam toward the noise. It wasn't on the counter by the cake, however; it was in the middle of the room, where my garbage bag had become an animate thing, leaping and scuttling about the kitchen.

A rat large and brash enough to cause all that commotion isn't the kind to run away from an argument, so I figured on shooting the entire affair, and never mind what the birdshot did to the floor. But just then the bag suddenly stilled and from a hole in its side emerged an exquisite little ermine, pure white except for the half-inch of black at the tip of its tail. It sat up and gazed unblinkingly into the light. I turned it off—the moon was bright, and I was struck with the urge to let the animal see me too—but when I did, it slipped back into the bag, and soon it was bouncing wildly around the room again. After a couple of minutes it stopped and the little fellow exited, vanishing under the stove and out the hole for the water pipe.

I was delighted by the visit. The next day I looked up *ermine* in an encyclopedia and discovered that my guest had been a "least weasel,"* the smallest wild carnivore in North America and by its size, a female. For the last couple of nights I've put out a bit of food before bed, but she hasn't returned.

*That's all an ermine is—a weasel that turns white in winter. My entire anatomy does the same thing but without any increase in value.

A Volunteer Fire Department report read out at last night's monthly dinner listed "two grass fires, one ambulance call, and one skunk removal."

BANNERS MADE OF SKY

The spruce live on
a crooked hill beyond
our crooked stream.

78

Sometimes mornings wind
make metal music in
the low, stiff branches
loggers hate. Or, higher,
soft, unurgent songs.

Our saws snort noisy
shapes of smoke
that rise to open places
through million-folded lace.

Always needles drizzle,
and broken panes
of light. They come
together falling, earth
before they touch.
The spruce succumb with
bravest grace, like yeomen
pledged to die for some
cold king—come twisting down
with banners made of sky
unfurling over them.

You approach a mature spruce warily. It bristles with bare,
steel-stiff limbs, hundreds of them, from the ground to the
height of a man's reach. They tear, gouge, scourge, impale.
They are naked and brittle because the heavy, inter-
laced boughs high above make a night in which the lower
branches cannot live.

The saw throbs and mutters, its oily chain idling along
the bar, the teeth fresh-filed, hungry. To drop a spruce—to
get at the base of the thick gray-brown trunk—you must cut
your way close enough; you must walk into the bristling

limbs and stiff-armed arc the saw from the ground to a point above your head. Then again and again, the machine smoking and howling now, limbs rat-tat-tatting off the trunk ten to a second. Sometimes the saw kicks back, a too-loose chain leaps off the bar, a bow-bent limb snaps slashing free.

Two cuts should drop the tree. Make the first one half an inch too deep, though, and the tree will close itself on the wound and trap the saw, stilling the chain. There's little power in the things, just biting, murderous speed. Sometimes wedges driven into the cut are enough to free it; sometimes it takes unbolting the saw from the bar, hooking up a spare, and making a fresh cut.

The falling's almost never clean. In all the spruce lots we have worked, the trees are close; any one is wed to half a dozen more. Severed from its base, a tree will likely twist away from where it's meant to drop, ladder its way down the row raining limbs and needles, or worse, lean menacing, the upper boughs caught fast. "Widow-makers" they're called. Forget in the drone and rattle of the work that you've left one hanging and it can pay you back, come whispering down behind you on a puff of breeze, inch loose over hours from neighboring boughs. Last year a local logger's spine was crushed that way. Another fellow caught one from behind that drove his face into the saw.

Limbing out is next. The mills demand that even smallest branches be cut flush to the trunk. You work along the fifty or so feet of fallen tree, the saw cocked inches from your leg, the branches fat and supple with life, resisting you. Cut free they make all movement difficult, like walking hip-deep against a heavy current. All spruce loggers have scarred knees from lurching into saws. You push ahead, never slowing, because you earn practically nothing working at a comfortable pace. The suburban homeowner cutting logs for the fireplace has his saw sharpened once or twice a season. We sharpen ours two or three times a day.

The limbing done, you block the bare trunk into four-foot lengths, give or take no more than an inch, shut down the saw and then with a tool much like a baling hook, you hump the blocks into piles along the edges of a row and drag the bigger branches off. If all goes well—it never does—it takes two days to clear the average row. Then you bring the tractor and the pulp cart in. The cart will hold a full cord or more if a man has strength enough to stack the blocks that high. Green and full of oozing sap, some weigh two hundred pounds. Somewhere along the row you've left a stump an inch too high The loaded cart hangs up; the tractor's spinning wheels mire axle-deep in a foul-smelling mix of mud and rotting boughs. So you dig and curse and know the load's got to come back off, the stump trimmed down, the whole back-breaking job repeated.

It may be half a mile out to the road, much of it a gantlet of bullying limbs. Once there, you take up the hook again, pull down the blocks, re-stack them so the mill can take their measure and pay you for your pulp—thirty dollars per cord, a pile four feet high, four feet deep, eight feet long. Less taxes, $3.50 to the state, the cost of gas and oil, the payments and repairs on tractor and saw, the shredded clothes, the agony. If I am honest in my calculating, I discover that I've earned about three dollars an hour. For what an industry study has classified as probably the most taxing, dangerous occupation in the United States.

But we have stood, my sons and I, and studied the long, long rows of spruce stacked at roadside, and we have swelled with knowing that most men wouldn't last a day at what we do. I'd go back to cutting spruce tomorrow if I weren't bedeviled by the silly ethic that a person's supposed to amount to something more than a cutter of pulpwood for the mills. I'd go back for the smell of fresh-dropped spruce, for the sound and feel of a howling saw in my hands, for the wild risk of it.

## LOGGING NIGHTS

I drove up on to State land this afternoon
and stopped and played the radio awhile,
oldies, songs we used to dance to
when cars had dimmer switches on
the floor. The shadow of a cloud turned
the meadow blue,
then freed it back to yellow.

It took me to how Jimmy Hamm said he
cut pulp by moonlight, the wash
of it waking him, how he'd fire up his saw
in all that silence, the light just strong
enough to flash from
the oily bar, smoke the color of a shadow.

We'd talked from truck to truck heading
different ways along the fire road out
of Clapper Hollow, and it wasn't any more
than that til now, ten years later,
Nat Cole forever dead but doing "Unforgettable,"
I see him out along some half-cut row
in all that killing tangle, lost
in the howling revery of his saw, and it hits
me that there had to be more to it
than using up some moonlight dropping spruce.

Today the doctor told me, "If you don't think splitting wood
is giving you enough of a workout, do five minutes of exercise every day. You know, lie down on the carpet in the living room and..."

"I don't have a carpet. I don't even have a living room,"
I said.

"Well," he responded. "just lie on the bare floor some-where. You look rugged enough."

"I don't have a floor."

"How in the hell can you not have a floor?" he demand-ed. "You mean you just walk in the door and...fall through? You end up back outside?"

"No," I said. "I have a sub-floor, but it's not nailed down all the way, so it's kind of like a trampoline. I have to shuf-fle across it or I keep flying up in the air. Can you recom-mend any bouncy kinds of exercises?"

He told me that I was the fourth person from Gilead he'd treated that week and that all of them were terribly healthy but none had made any sense. "I hope to God I never have to make a house call there," he said. Which is approximate-ly the sentiment that the sheriff's department has expressed about the town. Last Halloween we heard a deputy over the scanner call back to headquarters, "I ain't going into that crazy place without a backup."

We are forever misunderstood. There was no violence in Gilead that night, just three young fellows with no pants on going down the road eating apples.

WHAT YOU DO ON A MOUNTAIN

What you do on a mountain
is walk out naked in the night
and swim a cold new sea of hay.

Or play Ophelia in
your stream. Lie back and let
the current swing your arms
toward Spain like wavering weeds,
young water choke
your drowning song.

*83*

Give names of stars to stones, and
try green thorns beneath
your thumb. In May grass
turn and watch the bruises
of your footsteps heal.

Remind gnarled apple trees
to bear, the geese to halve
October's moon.

For any reason, dig.
Cut through the matted sod,
the clay, the ochre dirt.
Disintegrate the shale
with your long bar.
Inch down to where the earth
is gray and dead, to where
the hole is deep enough.

❧

SHALE

This was ocean once. The shale
is ocean-colored,
blue and gray and green and flat
like a sea.
A million years ago, mollusks swam
across its night.

Their fossils are printed in the shale
as clearly as
these words. I think of them drifting
down, away from the sun,
of the cataclysmic ebb, the new light,
of sudden islands.

Of what is left, the shale walls
that won't come down
until another ocean climbs these slopes
and new life swims
our fields. Not even then.

I'm too old to make it all the way up at a run, but earlier this evening I tried anyhow. Fixed my sights on a fence post near the top of the rise and nearly got there before my lungs gave out. I halted, puffing and blowing, just shy of where Clapper Hollow forks off from the blacktop. The hamlet lay below me. How pretty it looked at that hour, softly gray in the dusk, the mercury lights from far farms winking on, lamps showing at windows, the road empty of traffic.

There was the old ballfield where our horses over the years have worn a perfect oval. Beyond it the cemetery, where Charlie will be buried when the frost is out of the ground. The creek was full and rushing at the foot of the hill, boiling through the narrows, then spreading for a stretch before the high banks hemmed it in again. Its sound came mumbling up to me.

I wished aloud that it were mine to keep—the glow of lamps at evening, the pounding stream, the empty, winding road. I heard a faint, raucous cry. A mallard, barely visible against the darkening sky and darker hills, was looking for still water. His flight was confused, indecisive. The night baffled him; it was late for such seeking.

It doesn't require a heavy snowfall for deep drifts to form. I used to think otherwise, that drifts were correlative to blizzards, their sweep and depth and bulk the residue of great storms. But that is not necessarily so. It is wind that matters.

Not the scuddy kind of blow that makes sudden spiraling apparitions in open fields and momentary white-outs on a stretch of road, but a low, determined wind one cannot walk against. Such a wind can find in a scant three to four inches of dry powder enough snow, given appropriate terrain, to obliterate the work of plows and shovels in just moments.

I have watched the wind close this road, and the town's small plow open it, and the wind begin to close it again before the vehicle's taillights were out of sight. The high-shouldered haylot that makes up the entire horizon to the north provides a long, sloping plane down which the unimpeded wind gathers force, pushing before it every loose, uncertain flake, until there is not the faintest sign of Arabia Road at its foot, no evidence, except for the top of a fence post here and there, that I or anyone else has ever passed this way.

Isolation can thrill the imagination. Many mornings I have looked out on a world whose character has so altered in the night that I have felt pleasantly disoriented, unrooted from a particular time, with no proof anywhere on my drifted-over land of *now*. But it can also affect the mind in dark ways; it can be disturbing, frightening, especially with the onset of age.

I'm less than two thousand feet from a blacktop road, a five-minute hike when this narrow lane is clear. Even when it's not, traversing the drifted-over stretch between here and there on snowshoes is easy enough. Before the town conceded that there was indeed a year-round taxpayer up in Arabia and began to plow, snowshoes were regular footgear. I've hiked in on them with a stack of 2 x 4's on my shoulder or towing a hundred and fifty-pound tank of propane or with both arms full of groceries. I never thought anything of it, other than priding myself about being tough as blazes, bordering on invincible.

Since then, since the coming of plows and black wires that connect my cabin to the world beyond, snowshoes have mainly lost their utility. I use them for play now, for hikes in the woods with the dog and once in the midst of a blizzard for a trek to the top of the haylot, simply to discover what it would be like to stand exposed, facing that blinding howl. A week ago, when I drove off for the afternoon knowing it would snow before night, I neglected to put the snowshoes in the back of the car.

It was late when I returned and cold, at least fifteen degrees below zero. In the headlights I could see that the road was drifted with new snow. I mistook its depth, however, pulled down on the lever that kicked the vehicle into four-wheel drive, and plunged ahead. I covered maybe fifty feet before the Jeep became hopelessly stuck. I'd have to hike in, a shopping bag in one hand, a small suitcase in the other.

The dog ran on ahead. Even she had trouble, alternately bounding and sinking past her belly. Then she was gone in the darkness, heading toward home. With every step I sank past my knees. It takes enormous effort to walk in snow this deep; it is far more taxing than walking upstream against a heavy current of the same depth. There's little give to it. One begins to flounder, to gasp for breath. I wasn't even certain I was on the road anymore. It had become part of everything else. I knew only that it was getting deeper. And then I was in snow past my waist. In the attempt to struggle free and push on, I fell forward, letting go my burdens, flailing for balance.

My face was buried. When I thrust my arms down to push back, to lift my head and upper body, they met with nothing but yielding snow. Suddenly, I was in terrible trouble, winded, heart pounding, unable to keep my face free for more than scant seconds at a time. And had I wind and heart enough left to shout, there was no one to hear me.

In another field in another January, this time under a late, low sun, the same thing had happened. I was years younger and only a few yards from a firmly packed-down trail. But I remember imagining what a stricken member of a herd must sense, through the heaving vapor of my breath perceiving a hundred of me flying over the snow, never looking back.

Twisting and straining, I managed to roll over. Had the effort failed, I don't think I could have tried a second time. I lay there, still buried to the waist, and let my breathing slow. The cold hadn't penetrated yet; under me the snow was soft, comfortable. I put my head back, spread my arms wide. It was not an act of resignation, of philosophical calm. It was more the response of a swimmer trapped beneath his depth, who, struggling free and bursting to the surface, knows in that moment that breath is a miracle and does not strike for shore but treads water in an ecstasy of gratitude.

The mountain sky was very clear. I lay there looking up at stringy clusters of stars, trying to remember names of constellations. There was the Big Dipper, beyond its handle the brilliant star Arcturus, and, I think, Ursa Minor, the little bear. The rest were nameless to me, and that was momentarily troubling: that a serious student of mythology could not single out the mythical creatures that thronged above him in the night.

Looking back over the notes I scribbled later that evening, I come across this passage: "There are times when the mind is suddenly a-swirl with *narrative*, the passion to tell. We will never discover where it comes from, although it may be the one truly knowable thing about being human. An hour ago, I lay in a snowbank wanting nothing more than to tell my children how I died, its particular steps, and what of our life together had fled through my mind in the process. Again out of nowhere, a folksong I used to sing to them came to mind, 'Go Tell Aunt Rhody.' And then a couple of lines from a Raymond Carver poem written just after he'd been told he had terminal cancer—about how he would start that day to relish things he hadn't noticed before."

I knew out there in the snow that I wasn't going to die; these are simply notions that fly to mind when for a moment or so there are no preoccupations, when one is catching his breath, gathering strength. My hands were getting cold. I hadn't even thought to put on gloves for the hike. It was finally anger more than cold, though, that yanked me out of revery and free of the drift. Anger with my body, how it had waited, aging into weakness, for this perfect opportunity to betray me. I dug myself out with numbing fingers, cursing aloud the snow, the car, my stupidity—no snowshoes, gloves, flashlight—and found my fence, working along it hand over hand for two hundred yards or so until I hit clear road again.

### How Barns Go Down

Secretly and creaking slow
as ancient pachyderms go down
a vacant barn will go.
One to a winter,
eight winters in a row,
some empty-stanchioned place
has knelt
beneath a weight of snow.

It was murderously hot this afternoon, so I went for a swim toward six in the old quarry behind Bouton's farm and got caught at it by some strange, shouting fellow who ordered me off the place. It's impossible to settle a difference reasonably between two people when only one of them has his pants on. Your adversary has every advantage. But I wasn't willing to flee naked across Bouton's pasture either, so the two of us stood there and traded threats while I fumbled my way into my clothes.

I was still feeling stirred up when I ran into Bobby, who said he was on his way up the hill to steal some beehives and had figured on hiding them on my place, so I might as well give him a hand.

"What do you know about bees?" I asked him.

"I read somethin' about them once," he said.

"That makes one more thing you've told me that I don't believe," I said.

"You worry too much," he observed.

"Well," I said, "I want to know how you figure on carrying off a bunch of beehives without wearing any netting or gloves. You could get killed doing that."

"Said in this book they don't bother you at night," Bobby explained.

"I never heard that," I said, "and if I read a book that said sharks don't bite at night, I wouldn't jump into a pondful of them either."

By this time we were deep in the woods. Bobby pulled off and pointed to a break in the trees. I could see in the dusk the outline of perhaps half a dozen hives. I followed him through the thick brush. We stopped about twenty feet short of the clearing. "No sign of life," Bobby said. "Either they're all sleepin' or they've gone off somewheres."

He pushed through the thicket and approached the nearest hive. "I don't think you ought to touch that thing," I said. But he'd already yanked off the top and started to peer inside.

I've never seen as many bees in my life! Out they boiled, angry as rattlesnakes, the whole black raging cloud of them after Bobby's hide. He went off through the woods in a terrible hurry. I lost sight of him in a second or two, but I could hear his progress. Between his howls and branches breaking and the little rock slides he'd started, anyone could've stuck to his trail. Then I started catching it, too. A couple of them got inside my shirt and raised some hell and another one stung me just under the nose. I plunged off into a black-berry patch and got mauled even worse.

I met up with Bobby a few minutes later out on the road by the truck. He looked an awful mess, leaves and burdocks and twigs clinging to his hair and clothes, and his face already beginning to swell up. "I thought you said . . ." I began to say. But he cut me off: "I don't need any of your smartass schoolteacher stuff about bees and sharks or what-ever you were gonna say."

When I got back to the cabin I dug out a book about bees, and it said that if you cross Cyprians with Egyptians, you get a strain that's "so spiteful and vicious they have to be watched from a distance." So I figure that's the kind we got into and we should have checked on their ancestry before we tried to steal them.

## CULLEY'S DOG

Culley's dog is dead. I come down the mountain on
a Friday night to shoot a little pool, and quote
the-best-damn-friend-I-ever-had is dead again.
He says its father was pure wolf. Our wolves
don't have to breed; they've been flowing thin
and trackless for a hundred years out there beyond
the farthest light. Only liars see them,
except when they come in for easy kills,
when Culley's tears begin to smell like blood,
and then they lope out of the shadow of
the woods and cross the county road and crouch
outside the Rainbow door.

"You make me sick," he tells the stool his son
abandoned half an hour ago. He turns back to
the smoky light, the Country Renegades packing up
their instruments, and sets the story loose
a final time, the ghost of a hound by now,
bounding up and down the bar with Culley's heart
clamped in its jaws.

Then someone says, "You shot that goddam dog
ten years ago," and Culley spins around
half-falling off his stool, his face the wet-gray
color of a lie, and I see wolf
breath rising past the window in the door.

A strong dawning—blue, crackling clear, etching vividly the far mountains and casting in sharp relief each stalk, twig, half-buried sign of life projecting from the fresh snow. I strapped on snowshoes and set out up the road for the woods; then I looped along the ridge and back down to my stream. (Mine indeed. Least of all things is moving water ownable.) A couple of rabbits had preceded me to this shimmeringly beautiful place. Their tracks pocked the snow, crossed the frozen stream and disappeared into the underbrush. Back from the banks, laden spruce boughs stirred by a low wind had fanned angel wings in the whiteness, and just beyond the bend was a brown-bellied stretch of open water, clear and noisy as only winter water is. I walked back upstream and found that if I crouched I could hear between gusting surges of wind the current gurgling along under the ice. I mused for a bit about how fine it would be to share this moment with someone; then feeling mindlessly elated, set out across the stream.

Falling in with snowshoes on is complicated; it's nothing like the neat, posthole plunge that happens when you're in

92

boots. These fool contraptions took me down with implacable slowness. I fancy that I looked as tragic and forsaken as a torpedoed ship sliding under the waves. Toward the last I toppled over backwards, grabbing at the empty air, into the deepest part of the flow.

I can't think of a better way to clear one's head of extraneous nonsense than to sit waist-deep in a mountain stream in February. Clergymen and politicians should be made to do it regularly. I couldn't get up. The snowshoes were cocked at an impossible angle; when I attempted to heave my bulk forward, they threw me emphatically back. To unfasten the bindings I'd have to plunge most of my upper half under the rippingly frigid water. Eventually, that is what I did. But first I sat there for a span of maybe two minutes and laughed. I didn't choose to laugh; it simply welled forth of itself, untinged by bitterness or rue.

Probably too much of this kind of thing would wear a man down to weeping. I don't mean just the falling into icy water; I mean meeting oneself in some mortifying circumstance like this, where all the silly disguises of dignity and self-importance are revealed in a shocking moment for the emperor's garments they really are, and we are forced to bite down on a hard and awful and finally very funny truth: that of all creatures on God's chilly earth, we are doubtless the most ludicrous.

I just watched a buckwheat fly expire, and it came to mind that maybe death isn't so mysterious a thing after all. The fly had come to its dying time and had done what it was supposed to do on this Tuesday in early November, along with so many of its fellows.

I've wished these pesky insects dead a thousand times and have tried all fall to hurry them to it with chemicals and frenzies of swatting. But I got to watching this one fly tonight, and it was worth having him around for what he took me to reconsidering. The fly was buzzing directly above my little table, just within the arc of light from the lantern. He went around and around in the same slow circle, as if he was preoccupied with something pretty deep, the way a person will wear a path in a carpet walking out a problem.

Then, when he was maybe two feet over my coffee cup, he stopped. I don't mean stopped circling; I mean stopped living, cashed in his chips, plopped directly into my coffee, and floated there looking in the dim light like a little raisin. In these situations—and they occur regularly in these parts— it's customary to fish the insect out and flip it to the floor. But when I did so, I saw dead flies all around me. I'd swept up only yesterday, so these fellows all had to have died sometime tonight, maybe a hundred or more of them.

Which is what put me to thinking that what's born at a certain time is just as naturally going to die at a certain time, no matter what church he may belong to or how many laps he can do in the pool; and that this part of life's business is no more mysterious than growing whiskers. Maybe that fly was a Methuselah, but I doubt it. The chances are he was just standard issue, no older or smarter than any of the others littering my cabin floor.

I don't know what has pushed us so far off from our natural connection with this cycle—what makes us think we're so different from buckwheat flies and not wired up to last just so long and no longer. Dying wouldn't be nearly as confusing or downright terrifying if we stopped to figure that most of the people who were hatched out on a Tuesday in November of a certain year should be getting ready to make a few preoccupied circles and simply stop buzzing, and even more important, that we shouldn't waste the time we have in between one act and the other trying to buzz any louder or fancier than all the rest of the bunch. It all comes down, finally, to falling and, I hope, being good and dead before we hit.

## THIS UNEVEN PLACE

Four gravestones stand in this
uneven place. They're tilted all
the same, as if I'd caught
them frozen in a game of Giant Steps.
The vandalizing frost had pushed
the others down. The shallow dates
are gloved in moss and cracks break names
across. I cannot read whose bones
are here, what ounceless puffs of dead.

A shale wall has kept the woods away.
Odd that random-piled stones have stayed
so diligently propped, while from
these rakish monuments all vigilance
has dropped.

The birds sang about spring this morning. It's a quite distinctive chorus, although I don't recognize the soloists, just the rising, sunny-toned noises of the song. It's unlike that of the peepers, who sing somewhat damply about the gamble involved in being as ephemeral as a frog. Often lately I've studied the haylot, because more so than the leafing of trees, the greening of haylots reassures me. A month hence and its southeastward-facing slope will close its winter wounds. The ruts chewed deep into its tundra-like surface by mired vehicles will fill themselves. The falsely resolute tracks of snowmobiles will leave no lasting marks at all, not even slightest, although they have chewed their way up the steepest slope, biting with their black cleats, warming the snow with their noisy frictions, so that it melts and refreezes into fossilized perfections, evidence that something unreckonable still comes in the night, seven million years after the last nightlurker is supposed to have lain gently down in a stiffening swamp to die.

So I stare, knowing that given good weather, enough rain but not too much, this sweeping, high-ridged land will be green and flowing like gently stirred water in six weeks; and that by the end of June the grass will be considered hay and will be cut and raked and compressed into forty-pound bales and stored in oven-hot mows by boys whose shoulders and arms will ache and itch from the throwing and stacking.

Moss and lichen will color the underside of my woods, finding root or rebirth on damp rocks and rotting blow-downs. Some will turn amber and pink and grizzled gray, fragile colors, and some will go to blues and purples. I love to look at but not touch lichen. It never feels the way one thinks it will.

Dear friend, I could not catalogue in ten years the forms of life here on my small patch of land. Just tonight an insect crawled across my thumb, a winged creature with an elongated body and an onyx-black head. I wondered where it had been sleeping until this third day of spring—possibly within my walls or perhaps between bark and wood until I carried his home into the cabin and dumped it in the wood-box by the stove. I became more interested in this cellophane-winged Lazarus than in the New York Times, across which it crawled from my thumb.

The moon is coming to the full. It has cleared the raking tips of the highest hemlocks and looks down in dubious majesty at this bleak, snow-covered patch of planet whereon I and a red squirrel and a tense, distrustful chipmunk make out homes. I had intended to hike up the road but felt drawn on this moonbright, blueskinned night to the haylot. I walked along the stonewall fence, looking back with rushes of curiosity and affection at my cabin, watching it diminish

96

into near impalpability, becoming only a silver wraith of spuming woodsmoke and a yellow-gold glow at the window, and I thought about how beckoning such a sight would be to a cold and weary traveler.

The climb grew steeper and my breathing quickened long before I reached the ridge. The mountains seemed the world's rim. In the trick played by winter air and moonlight, it seemed fabulous that beyond the farthest night-tinged hill the earth continued. I don't know why I started running, but I doubt I've moved as fast in fifteen years. Across the top of the haylot, then quartering down the slope, sensing I was running maybe a hundred miles an hour, I loped pell-mell over tussocks and chuck holes, thinking I don't care if I trip, I'm unhurtable on this night, within these minutes; I'm not just an old-muscled, stiff-jointed schoolteacher running down a hill at midnight; I've absorbed a grace, a wild fluidity, from living here.

I leaped the ditch at the foot of the field, came to a stop in the middle of the road, leaned back and hollered for all I was worth. It was for no one to hear. I've done that before—bellowed at the top of my lungs from one spot on this mountain or another. It's easy to forget that built into our design is the need to holler.

Last Saturday, I attended a one-day fly fishing course at a sporting goods shop not far from here. One leg of the course dealt with entomology, the other with technique. It occurred to me halfway through the first part that I had drifted hopelessly away from the practical business at hand when, with the ten or so other students scribbling busily away, I fell to musing in response to the speaker's comments. He was a wiry, bearded little fellow of about forty who, he confessed, was "obsessed with the sport." It soon became apparent, though, that for him it was not truly a sport at all but a

97

noble passion. He talked knowingly about certain insects, detailing their identifying features and behavior. It was an exacting lecture, not even faintly poetic. Yet when he charted the life cycle of the mayfly, I'd put down my pen and begun to ponder the wonder, the beauty of it—how they come from under stones in the cold belly of a stream and rise toward the light, shedding their girdling exoskeletons, and at the surface, given the sun's warmth, their tight-packed wings unfold, open, dry. How glorious that must feel!

And then they fly, the survivors, and rest on tree branches until some minute arc of instinct pushes them off into the air again, their wings now turned from dun to shimmering iridescences, the males to couple with females over the stream and die, falling to the surface to be eaten by hungry trout. The females will lay their eggs on the water and follow the same fate. All in a day. "You can see them in the air evenings, whole clouds of them. It looks like they're dancing sometimes," the instructor said. The subject was how to imitate them with dryflies, how to mimic such a miracle, how to fool the fish.

I couldn't get that talk out of my head; I lay there in the dark that night thinking about how we long ago lost any sense that we too figure in a cycle that began with the very first of our species, and also about my setting off that morning to learn a way to catch trout and returning wrung with passion and renewed astonishment about how beautiful is this world. I thought for a couple of days that I should write a note to Joe Alberico and tell him what a rich thing it was for me to sit through his talk. But I knew it would be taken wrong; he'd figure me for some kind of sissified nut he'd never want to fish the same stream with.

In the middle of his lecture, he'd stopped suddenly and said, "Thursday I caught the biggest damn brown I'll ever catch. She went twenty-six inches, weighed seven pounds. I been flyfishing for twenty years. Finally, there she was." That was it; he'd gotten out what any avid fisherman would find it irresistible to brag about, especially to an audience made up of other fishermen. Then he went directly back to talking about insects, distributing handouts, answering questions. After maybe half an hour, he stopped again: "I don't make any money doing this. I do it because if you got to fly-fish, I'd just as soon it was me who taught you.

"You and me, we have to save trout, not kill them. For our kids, not just us. That brownie. You think I wasn't tempted? I haven't kept a single trout for over 17 years, not even to eat. But here's this giant. And you know, you tell your friends and they say, 'Sure, Joe, sure—a twenty-six-inch brown, hah-hah.' So I ain't gonna stand here and tell you I didn't nearly break my vow. But I'm also thinking, You kill her, you're going to know it all your life. I had her in my arms, still in the water, like this [he cradled his arms in front of him, as if he were rocking and infant] for it must've been three minutes, just looking at her, knowing what I had to do but hating like hell to do it. Then I took out the hook, kissed her on the head, and let her go."

Later, when we were standing outside for a minute during a break, he said to me, "You know, I bet I stopped four times for coffee and a cigarette on the way home, and I'd sit there in the car just smiling and smiling and thinking about that damn fish."

I didn't tell him about my poem, a favorite, about catching the first bluefish of the year. It begins,

> I come back Aprils,
> a hook for a question. . .

And it ends
> I kiss the snout,
> half-wanting it
> to bite my lips away.

It's a terrible shame that a man can't say all that much to another man about such moments. Because I'll bet that somewhere in him Joe would love knowing that he'd so touched another male, and I can't find a way to tell him.

🐾

## LUNGINGS OF THE HEART

A trout has struck my thready worm,
a second little fish, the
other silver-swimming in last light.
The bobber writes brave circles on the
shadowed pool.

I cannot see the filament
that runs from him to me. We're joined
invisibly across this moment of
a stream by nothing but
the lungings of a tiny, wild heart.

🐾

Just west of Richfield Springs yesterday afternoon a trooper pulled me over to explain somewhat apologetically that I had whipped past his radar gun going seventy. I felt no urge to argue; I told him only that I was heading for a funeral down the line and also that I thought he should be wearing a longer coat to keep his revolver from freezing up. I pulled back out on Route 20 and put the incident from mind. I was going down to Middleburgh to pay my last respects to Johnny on this bitter cold February afternoon, after all, and so I began to concentrate on fitting myself into the floor-length mantle of grief that one is supposed to wear until such solemnities are over.

Except I knew this to be impossible. I've tried at least twenty times in my life to give myself wholly over to public grieving, and never once have I made it from start to finish without wandering off into one of those little rooms of the mind that if their contents were exposed would get you dragged outside and told never to come back again. It isn't that I'm too shallow or self-absorbed to feel deep grief. It's that its shape is never distinct, unless perhaps it is the shape of distraction itself. Too clearly have I heard the whispers of stiff clothing, the far sounds of the world outside, or have fallen into study of a profile or noted the closet smell of people gotten up in outfits they haven't worn since the last time they mourned, or even let the lyrics from a song sing themselves in my head. And always I have scanned the room, the church, the temple and thought, I am the only one among these congregants whose heart does not truly ache.

It was dusk by the time I turned onto Route 10 at Sharon Springs. Billie Holiday was doing "Just One of Those Things," and I knew she'd swing from there into "A Foggy Day in Londontown" and that it would be a clear, starbright night. The hills were going blue, lights coming on here and there, the road mostly empty. I tried concentrating on Johnny, but the only way I could hold to it was to begin telling him out loud what I saw, racing down a country road in a pickup truck on my way to say goodbye to him.

The double doors of the funeral home swung open just as I was reaching for the handle. There was a woman on each door, one of them in a black pants suit, the other, younger and prettier, in a blouse and skirt. She, I noticed when I got inside, held a cigarette cupped behind her in her free hand. "Peer Gynt" was fluting softly from a hidden speaker. The older woman nodded me toward what I think is called a "viewing room" that opened off the parlor and which was ranked with rows of brown metal chairs, half of them occupied.

The coffin was at the very front, set apart by twenty feet or so from the first row of mourners. The closed bottom half was draped with a large flag. I hadn't known til then that Johnny was an ex-serviceman. For that matter, I wasn't even sure that it was Johnny in the casket. It didn't look much like him. I stood there wondering if I'd entered the wrong chamber, and the longer I wondered, the more worried I became, for I had slipped into what I imagined to be the posture of a grief-stricken friend, eyes downcast, hands clasped behind my back, standing in the pooled shadow of memories made poignant by the music, the bright profusion of flowers crowding the front of the room, and the top half of the propped, still fellow in the casket.

It couldn't be Johnny; a dozen furtive glances around the room turned up not one familiar face. I was in the wrong room, possibly even in the wrong funeral hall. I was bringing my most earnest efforts at grieving to bear on a total stranger, and by now everyone in the room knew that I was an imposter, one of those ghoulish people who come out of the night to warm themselves by the flame of others' sadness. I tiptoed out of the hall and across the wide parlor, imagined suspicion and resentment following me as I peered into one viewing room after another seeking a familiar face, a corpse resembling Johnny Delia. They were empty, every one.

I returned and stole a look at the memorial book propped on a stand by the door. But on its first page under the scrolled heading "In Memory of" the space was blank, and on the following pages not one mourner's signature was familiar to me. I wrote my name in the first free space. I wrote carefully, legibly, not the way I sign a check or a credit card voucher. Someday soon, possibly tomorrow, Johnny's common-law widow would study these pages, and it wouldn't do for it to look as if I'd attached no more importance to the moment than if I were signing for a couple of shirts.

102

Then I sat down near the back, figuring it probably was Johnny, if only because it wasn't anybody else.

Bobby came in about then and sat down next to me. He'd done the right thing—gone up and looked at the body in the coffin first. "Don't look much like him," he whispered.

"Got a ticket coming down," I whispered back.

"Son of a bitch," he said, shaking his head, meaning You try to do good and look what happens. A fat woman in a powder blue suit turned around and glared at us. Bobby isn't a good whisperer; you can hear him from about a hundred yards away. "How old's John?" I said.

"Gotta be at least a year younger than me, and I ain't forty yet," he said. Then he worked it all out how he knew. Something to do with how Johnny's sister went to school with his wife, and she's a year younger than Bobby, and Johnny was at least a year younger than his sister because he was in a lower grade, unless he stayed back a couple of times, in which case he'd be Bobby's age just about. Still standing by the door, the younger woman took an enormous drag on a cigarette, her cheeks going so hollow from the effort that their insides nearly touched.

The room was filling up. Marshall came in and then Bing, along with all three daughters and Bonnie and his son-in-law Roger, and just after them the minister, who maybe you couldn't blame for not talking much about Johnny because he didn't know him and said so right at the start. Still, I do think he went off in some unlikely directions and that just a little bit about John, which he could have picked up without much trouble, would have been miles more interesting than the blather about Jeremiah and Thomas and then the Forty-second Psalm and then a windy parable about snowflakes and seeds and little children that got worse and worse as it went along. Bobby, though, began to cry softly to himself in the middle of it. He pulled out a handkerchief and blotted his eyes and cried a little more, and when the service was finally over and we got up to leave, I noticed a still-wet tearstain on the edge of his chair.

Out in the parlor people put on coats and stood in groups of four or five talking. The men especially seemed to take up twice the space they'd occupied sitting in the dim of the viewing room. Even this was part of it. A faint formality clung, a shared sense that it would violate the delicacy of ceremony to clap one's hat on and walk out into the night. It was a last chance to participate in the society of bulky, close-cropped, reticent men held together for a final few minutes by the need to speak tenderly, eloquently about the fellow lying in the next room dressed in a brandnew plaid flannel shirt, who looked older and different and terribly dead.

It is impossible, though, ever to say the right thing or even to come close. "Sure don't look like Johnny in there," Bobby said again. "Looks way too old."

"He sure went fast. Shame he was so young though, terrible shame," Bing commented. His eyes were red. Johnny had been like a younger brother to him. When he called to tell me the news, he'd broken down; his daughter Lois had to take the phone.

On the way out of the viewing room I'd picked up one of those memorial cards with a prayer on the overleaf and facing that the deceased's name and birth and death dates. Hell, Johnny wouldn't have been thirty-seven until next November. Never mind that he'd adventured more than most who grew up here; it had been so clear coming across from Sharon Springs that I could make out every piece of stubble in a windswept cornlot a quarter-mile away and how the snow went from white to blue to purple as the light faded. I'd felt the same tingle I always feel when the mountains loom just past the turn above Richmondville. In the morning, I knew, I'd be able to tell early from the color of the sky how the day would be, the horse would nicker for his grain, the white ducks bob and preen in the pond. Oh, this is when it is, friend John, in the dark going home under every star you've ever larked and loved beneath, that suddenly I know how much I mourn for you.